THE DAVIS HOMESTEAD

THE DAVIS HOMESTEAD

A Farm Since 1680
in Lower Pawcatuck, Connecticut

A Collection of Writings

by John Lawrence Davis

Editor, 1986 Edition:
Emily H. Lynch

Editors, 2007 Edition:
James Boylan and Betsy Wade

all the best from Betsy + Jim
6/08

STONINGTON HISTORICAL SOCIETY
STONINGTON, CONNECTICUT

The Stonington Historical Society, P.O. Box 103,
Stonington, CT 06378
ISBN-13: 978-0-9794013-1-2
ISBN-10: 0-9794013-1-3

This publication was made possible, in part, by a
grant from the Connecticut Humanities Council.

*Photograph of Continental Marsh, Stanton-Davis
farm, by Fred E. Burdick*

CONTENTS

In Appreciation

The personal copy of the first edition of this book belonging to Emily Harrison Lynch of Stonington bears this inscription in a clear, firm hand:

> *To Emily Lynch*
> *Whose long, hard work on my manuscript made this book possible. Thank you so much.*
> *John L. Davis*

That edition, and this one, had a genesis almost thirty years ago. Mrs. Lynch, a stalwart of the Stonington Historical Society, learned in 1980 or so that there was a "mountain" of historical notes at the Davis Farm that would be worth researching. John Lawrence Davis, who was eighty-two in 1980, had kept a farm diary for decades and, for about twenty years, had been writing a narrative about his historic homestead. He had tried to interest two New England publishers, but nothing developed.

Mrs. Lynch, who was married to a retired naval officer and historian, Frank Lynch, was the ideal choice to take up the challenge. She had founded the Society's education committee, which brings local history to life in area classrooms. She was co-editor of *Stonington Graveyards, a Guide*, a difficult project published in 1980, which remains a benchmark for the Society.

Mrs. Lynch began visiting Davis, who was recently widowed, in his sitting room at the homestead a couple of hours at a time. This went on for more than four years, mostly in the winter. "There were piles of notes handwritten on lined notebook paper, and some typed by one of his granddaughters," Mrs. Lynch said in an interview in 2006. She took away Davis's sheets of writing for transcribing and also made notes on Davis's stories as they talked. Mrs. Lynch said she appreciated his sense of humor and they got to be good friends. Each typed portion was returned for Davis to approve.

In 1986, when everything was typed and organized, the Historical Society published it in typescript as a spiral-bound book. Davis died in 1989.

To recognize her creation of the education committee and her crucial role in two of the Society's books, as well as her many articles for the Society's publication, *Historical Footnotes,* the Society honored Mrs. Lynch in 1994 with the title Fellow of the Society and she was named Grand Marshal of its Independence Day parade in 2003.

For this new edition, Mrs. Lynch has offered information, support and advice. Readers will see afresh what can be achieved by a sustained collaboration by two hard workers.

ACKNOWLEDGMENTS

The editors of this new edition of *The Davis Homestead* have received invaluable assistance from many hands. We wish to offer special thanks to:

Fred E. Burdick, Stonington's town historian and vice president and treasurer of the Stanton-Davis Homestead Museum, whose searches in the homestead produced many of the family photographs published here for the first time, and whose own handsome photographs enrich the presentation.

John Whitman Davis, John Lawrence Davis's son, whose co-operation and information on his family, especially in identifying persons in photographs, have proved invaluable.

Laurie M. Rayner and her colleagues at the Connecticut Humanities Council, whose support made this publication possible.

The staff of the Stonington Historical Society, notably Mary Beth Baker, executive director, for support and advice; Anne T. Tate, librarian of the Richard W. Woolworth Library, and the library volunteers. We are also especially grateful for the support of the president of the Stonington Historical Society, Michael H. Adair, and the chair of its publications committee, Anne Connerton.

Professor Nancy H. Steenburg and Professor Emeritus Rudy J. Favretti of the University of Connecticut for their perceptive readings of the book's new introduction.

The Town of Stonington employees who helped immensely in our pursuit of historical records, notably Assessor Marsha Standish, the staff of the town clerk's office, and Joe Bragaw.

Michael J. Tranchida, city clerk of the City of New London, whose assistance enabled us to trace the farm's seventeenth-century records.

The skilled reference staff of the Westerly Public Library, which provided access to that library's rich resources and permitted us to use their photograph of the Clark Mill.

Jim McDonald, reference librarian, Connecticut College.

Carol Butler of the Brown Brothers photo agency, who tracked and found the originals of the Davis farm photographs shot about 1906.

Suzanna Tamminen, director and editor-in-chief of the Wesleyan University Press, who provided indispensable guidance on finding a printer for this book.

Jamie Trowbridge, publisher, and Debbie Despres of *Yankee Magazine*, for permission to publish their 1971 photos of the Davis farm.

FAMILY MEMBERS MENTIONED

John Lawrence Davis: Born December 3, 1898, died July 2, 1989. The author and narrator.

Sarah Shaw Davis: Born 1901, died April 7, 1979. The author's wife.

Alphonso Whitman Davis: Born February 20, 1861, died May 9, 1908. The author's father.

Ida May Palmer Davis: Born November 24, 1867, died March 20, 1908. The author's mother.

Marcia Louise Davis Gabrielsen: Born October 7, 1900, died February 24, 1990. The author's sister.

John Jeremiah Davis: Born June 16, 1854, died November 27, 1929. The author's uncle.

Elizabeth Hamilton Davis: Wife of John Jeremiah, the author's Aunt Bess.

Sarah Maria Davis, Born February 23, 1856, died 1944. Sister of John Jeremiah and Alphonso; the author's Aunt Sarah.

John Davis: Born April 11, 1808, died April 9, 1884. Father of John Jeremiah, Sarah Maria, and Alphonso Whitman Davis and grandfather of the author.

Phebe Mulford Davis Davis: Born February 2, 1824, died March 29, 1908. Mother of John Jeremiah, Sarah Maria and Alphonso Whitman and grandmother of the author.

John Davis: Born September 19, 1776, died April 21, 1864. Father of John Davis (1808-1884), great-grandfather of the author.

Sarah (Sally) Stanton: Born July 20, 1776, died September 6, 1861. Mother of John Davis (1808-1884), great-grandmother of the author.

John Whitman Davis: "Whit," born August 3, 1924. Son of the author and Sally Shaw Davis.

Hazel Thompson Davis: Born October 17, 1925, died November 7, 1984. First wife of John Whitman Davis.

Susan Davis, born 1946; **John Carter Davis**, born 1948; **Lawrence Malcolm Davis**, born 1958, and **Carolyn Davis**, born 1963, grandchildren of the author.

Note: With the author's consent, the editor of the 1986 edition changed "a few names."

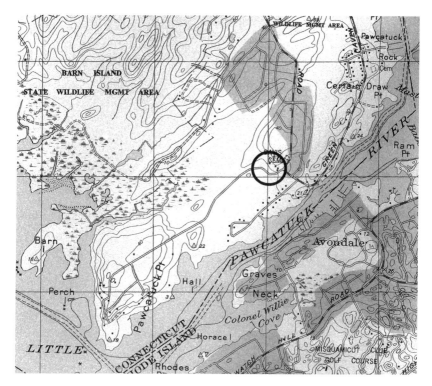

The historical boundaries of the Stanton-Davis farm lie in the area shown on the modern topographical map above, originally extending from near Thomas Stanton's trading post (upper right corner) to Pawcatuck (or Osbrook) Point at the bottom and Barn (or Stanton) Island on the left. The homestead is circled.

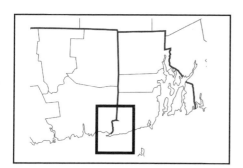

Left: The Stanton-Davis farm lies in Lower Pawcatuck, in the south-eastern corner of south-eastern Connecticut.

INTRODUCTION

John Lawrence Davis's memoir, *The Davis Homestead*, recounts half a century of life on a farm in Lower Pawcatuck, tucked into the southeast corner of the most southeasterly town in Connecticut, Stonington. This old farmer's recollections don't fall into such familiar genres of rural writing as musings by literary gentlemen in overalls or oral histories channeled by interviewers. What we read are John Lawrence Davis's own writings — prepared by a sympathetic editor, but with the farmer himself laying down the terms of discourse.

In straightforward, rambling, earthy, even harsh terms he recounts the practice and lore of family farming of an era, the twentieth century, now passed, with an eye on his farm's rich history and with warm affection for his family, the diverse and changing crew who came to work there, and his assortment of neighbors.

The Davis Homestead is no ordinary farm. It was one of the earliest granted when English migrants settled Connecticut's eastern coast in the mid-1600s. Its centerpiece is a house built before 1700, perhaps as early as the 1670s, a durable structure expanded from time to time but never "rehabilitated" or emptied of its contents. The house lies on land that has remained productive through more than three centuries of prudent cultivation and is now protected forever from development. The fields still present an unbroken vista from the old house toward the sea.

The farm's history has yet to be told in full. John Lawrence Davis retells what was handed down to him through his family; his son, John Whitman Davis, has provided additions; writers and reporters have romanticized it. As customarily retold, the story is a potpourri seeded with notable names and legendary events — Thomas Stanton, the colonial trader and interpreter; the sachem Uncas; the mighty slave Venture; the Revolution; the War of 1812; the great storm of 1938.

But for most of its existence this was a farm much like any other large farm, sustained only by the endless daily work and sweat of plowing, harvesting, canning, sawing, feeding, milking, slaughtering, fighting through the seasons, with weather or sickness or injury always threatening. And, as has been the case for centuries, the work done by the farm's women is often obliviously uncredited or undercredited. Humble stuff, except that it has gone on, all but uninterrupted, for more than three hundred years, adjusting only slowly to modern technology and convenience.

The farm lies just beyond the eastern outlet of Long Island Sound, at the end of the sheltered Connecticut coast; its marshes still produce their original crop of salt hay. Well before the English arrived, Native Americans communities lived at water's edge, harvesting shellfish and growing food. As it faces Little Narragansett Bay, the farm is partly shielded from the force of the Atlantic by the arm of Napatree Point reaching west from the Rhode Island barrier beaches, but the land remains vulnerable to the worst of storms.

The farm's most famous proprietor was the first, Thomas Stanton. An English immigrant, he abruptly appears in New England records in the mid-1630s, a youth already familiar with Native American languages. The Stanton family tradition is that he learned the languages on a long hike up from Virginia after he debarked. More likely, he was tutored by the seasoned Indian trader John Oldham, whose murder in 1636 touched off the bloody Pequot War.

Stanton's diplomatic and linguistic skills were called on continually in dealings with the tribes that contended with the English for control of New England over the next forty years; he was viewed as a firm but friendly go-between. At the farm, there is a table pointed out as the one on which Thomas Stanton in 1670 wrote the will of Uncas, sachem of the Mohegans and an ally of the English, an act memorialized in family tradition and by the historians Frances M. Caulkins and Richard Anson Wheeler.

Thomas Stanton settled in Hartford about 1636 and married Anna Lord, daughter of one of the founding families. In 1649, the General Court, the Connecticut colony's new governing body, authorized him to set up a trading post on the Pawcatuck, the river that ultimately became a boundary between Connecticut and Rhode Island. Stanton moved with his growing family — he and Anna eventually had six sons and four daughters — to Pequot Plantation, which embraced an area now containing the towns of New London, Groton, and Stonington.

The farm came into being in 1652. Frances M. Caulkins, in her enduring *History of New London* (1860), wrote that Pequot Plantation, in an array of land grants, in 1652 gave Stanton 300 acres at "Pawkatuck," directly south of his trading post. Records preserved by the city of New London, containing early Stonington land transactions, confirm the grant at "Pocatuck." A subsequent grant extended Stanton's holdings into the adjacent marshes and the "Hammackes," or mounds, rising from them.

Stanton settled his family in a house, now long vanished, near the trading post, about 1656. In the years that followed, he was a key figure in helping to mold and govern the new settlement that broke off from Pequot Plantation. For a time, the place was known as Southertown and was part of Massachusetts; Connecticut reclaimed the area and called it Mystic, and, ultimately, Stonington. After decades of dispute, the Pawcatuck River, bounding Stanton's farm on the east, became the Rhode Island line. Meanwhile, Stanton became an extensive landowner on both sides of the river, with grants and purchases in both Connecticut and Rhode Island. Further, he and his sons engaged in trade with Barbados, in the West Indies, a stopping place in the transatlantic slave trade.

The house that is now the hub of the farm is old; its exact age is not known. It has elaborate imported woodwork and other appurtenances of wealth, but it is not clear whether it was a fine house at the start or expanded into one as the Stantons prospered. John Lawrence Davis follows family tradition in saying that it was built in 1680 and expanded in 1752. The Historic American Buildings Survey, which

The original 1652 land grant of 300 acres in Pawcatuck to Thomas Stanton, as recorded in the Pequot Plantation records, now held by the City of New London.

analyzed it 1937, guessed that it was built in 1700. It has been generally known as the "Robert Stanton House," after Thomas Stanton's fifth son (1653-1724), its first long-term occupant.

In recent years, thanks to a Stanton family genealogist, Bernard John Stanton, Thomas Stanton's will was found in the Connecticut State Library in a section called "Private Controversy Collections." It was filed there because intra-family disputes kept it unsettled forty years, until 1718. The will was written in October 1677, little more than a month before Stanton died, in his sixties, unable to join the four sons who fought in 1675 and 1676 in King Philip's War, the conflict that confirmed the English conquest of New England. Finding in the will a reference to a "new house south of the old house" — the old house perhaps being the home near the trading post — Bernard Stanton developed the thesis that the house was built before Thomas Stanton's death, during the 1670s. The will confirms that the "new house" was the one given to Robert Stanton. Plausible as this contention appears, fuller substantiation must wait further scientific and historical analysis of the house itself.

The will elaborately divided the Stanton farm: Thomas Jr. was given 160 acres lying along the river; Daniel, 40 acres just to the south (and a hundred acres elsewhere); Robert and Samuel, a division of the rest of the unspecified property "where I now live," Robert specifically getting the "new house" and Samuel, the youngest, the right to improve his half. The farmland now had four owners, and was further subdivided with each generation, Connecticut having forbidden primogeniture in its legal code of 1650.

The farmlands were destined to remain in the hands of the Stantons for less than a century — three generations — after the death of the senior Thomas. By the middle of the eighteenth century, through diffusion and partition among large families, the original tract had become a patchwork. On the death in 1751 of Thomas Stanton, grandson of the original Thomas and proprietor of what was by then called in deeds "the Homsted farm," his elder son Robert (1716-1779) took charge of putting the pieces back together.

First Robert divided his father's property with his younger brother, the fourth Thomas (1729-1799), giving him the western portion of the farm (now absorbed into the Barn Island Wildlife Management Area); then he bought up the rights and holdings of his sisters. He also acquired from his second cousin, the third Samuel Stanton, 91 acres of upland and 13.5 acres of salt marsh for £7,866 in heavily depreciated paper, known as "Old Tenor bills of credit." Samuel may have sold his farm because he was going into military service; he died in action two years later at Crown Point, New York, during the French and Indian War.

Robert and Thomas meanwhile earned historical notoriety. The Stantons held Africans and Indians as slaves, and about 1754 Thomas, then twenty-five years old, acquired an African slave, about his own age, who been given the name Venture, and was a man of immense strength. A "Venture stone," purportedly weighing 442 pounds, which Venture is believed to have lifted and carried, is now set outside the old Robert Stanton house, although Thomas, not Robert, was Venture's owner.

According to Venture's autobiographical *Narrative*, neither brother treated him well or fairly. Robert borrowed Venture's saved-up earnings and gave him a note, which he later stole and tore up. Venture's wife, also purchased by Thomas Stanton, was set upon by Thomas's wife and later Thomas assaulted Venture as well. When Venture complained to a magistrate, the two brothers ambushed him on the road; he subdued them both.

To his relief, Venture was finally sold, about 1760, to Colonel Oliver Smith, who permitted him to purchase his freedom. Later, Venture bought a small farm near Thomas Stanton's place and, when he left Stonington, sold it to Stanton, his former owner. And it is the slave rather than his abusers whose reputation has survived into the twenty-first century.

In 1764 Robert Stanton took a step that he may have contemplated since his father's death more than a decade before. For whatever reasons — need of money, family disputes, distaste for farming — he moved away and let the old farm go. On October 24, 1764, in a transaction a family genealogist has characterized as a mortgage loan, he sold the farm's 450 acres to two moneyed men of Southold, Long Island, for £2,160 in the currency of the Province of New York. The next year the farm was rented to John Davis of East Hampton, Long Island (1723-1798), who put his 17-year-old son, John, in charge while he carried on his leather and shoe business. Eight years later, the elder John Davis bought the farm for £2,627, a modest enough markup.

The Davises, steady and patient, remained owners of the farm through eight generations. Unlike the Stantons, they were not public or military men; they stuck to the farm, scarcely noticing the salt water at their doorstep, nor indeed the world at large. In John Lawrence Davis's memoir, the two world wars of his own time receive less notice than the American Revolution or the War of 1812.

A strong family tradition declares that in the first years of Davis ownership, the harvest of salt hay from the farm's marshes was sold in 1775 to support Washington's Continental Army, then laying siege to Boston. The family has since known the site, lying south and west of the house, as the "Continental Marsh," or the "Continental." The name is now memorialized in the family's 1978 deed transferring the tract to a local land trust, the Avalonia (Mashantucket) Land Conservancy.

The younger John Davis followed acquisition of the farm by marrying Abigail Baker, from an East Hampton family. They ran the farm together for the next thirty-six years while raising seven children. When he died in 1809, this Davis left a portrait of the farm in his probate inventory: Besides the land, he listed a yoke of oxen, forty-three cattle of various ages, forty sheep, and ten hogs. In his will he provided that his widow would have a third of the estate, livestock of her choice, a "high case of drawers," the "Looking Glass, that hangs in the

The fourth John Davis in a studio portrait made by Leighton Bros. in Norwich, Connecticut; he was born in 1808 and died in 1884. He was the father of John Jeremiah, Alphonso Whitman, and Sarah Davis. Phebe Mulford Davis, their mother, married her second cousin John in 1851, and this may be a wedding portrait. The instructions for tinting it say, "Hair dark brown Eyes blue dress black Tint cheeks fill out shoulders."

west Great Room," a "Large Hand iron," a brass kettle, and, finally, firewood "cut and carted to the door" for life by two sons, John and Daniel.

The third John Davis, born in 1776, also enjoyed a long tenure. In 1804, he married Sarah Stanton, known as Sally, thus symbolically reuniting the two proprietary families, although Sally came from a branch that had not lived on the farm in generations. The neighborhood was full of Stantons; two of John's siblings also married into the Stanton family. John and Sally had six children, including the fourth John, born in 1808, John Lawrence Davis's grandfather. The farm prospered; the tax rolls for 1850 place the Davises among the ten wealthiest families in Stonington, with property assessed at $18,992. Sally died in 1861; John, in 1864.

The fourth John Davis married Phebe Mulford Davis, a second cousin, in 1851. He was known as a quiet, self-effacing man (perhaps accounting for his waiting until he was forty-three to marry). On his death in 1884, a pastor of the Congregational Church in Westerly recalled: "I can see him now, as he drove up to the steps of the church, a hale and strong man, with the color of health in his cheeks, and his whole countenance beaming with an expression of hearty good will to all around." He and Phebe had three children — John Jeremiah, Sarah Maria, and Alphonso Whitman.

On December 3, 1898, John Lawrence Davis, the farm's sixth John Davis, was born into a family that included his father, Alphonso; his mother, born Ida May Palmer in Norwich; his uncle, John Jeremiah, and John Jeremiah's wife, Elizabeth Hamilton Davis, who were childless; his unmarried aunt, Sarah Maria; and his grandmother, Phebe Mulford (Davis) Davis. His sister, Marcia Louise, was born less than two years later.

He has surprisingly rich memories of that household, which was to last only into his ninth year. In 1908, in quick succession he lost his grandmother, his mother, and finally his father, who attempted suicide after his wife's death and died in a Providence hospital at the age of forty-seven.

The three remaining — Uncle John Jeremiah (known as "Uncle John Jerry"); and his uncle's wife and sister, whom John Lawrence Davis remembers as "Aunt Bess" and "Aunt Sarah" — took over bringing up John Lawrence and Marcia Louise. Perhaps life on a farm had already conditioned the child to the realities of life and death, and while he recalls his father (and less so, his mother) fondly, he does not show evidence in the memoir that he believed his life was thrown off course.

Like many other farm boys, he attended school reluctantly and left early, at the age of sixteen, and in 1914 took over his share of managing the farm, a job that lasted fifty years. He kept a terse, episodic diary to remind himself of the cycles of planting and harvesting. One of its features was the record of the enormous quantities of manure that had to be hauled out at the end of each winter. Until he retired he rarely mentioned family in the diary.

He had a family nonetheless. By his early twenties, John Lawrence had met a young woman, Sarah Shaw, known as Sally, born in Scotland. They were married in 1921 and remained partners for fifty-eight years. They had one child, John Whitman (Whit), born in 1924.

In these years, the household comprised John Lawrence and Sally; young Whit; John Lawrence's Aunt Sarah; and Uncle John Jeremiah and Aunt Bess. Neither in his memoir or his diary does he note the subsequent deaths of his uncle or his aunts.

His sister, Marcia, whom John Lawrence apparently regarded without much affection, is also largely absent from his memoir, although she did more than her share of farm work and cared a dozen years for their Aunt Sarah after she was disabled in a farm accident. Aunt Sarah remembered Marcia gratefully in her will, and Marcia's nephew, Whit, recalls her as almost a second mother. After Sarah's death in 1944, Marcia was at last free to marry, did so, returning to the farm only when she and her husband were elderly.

John Lawrence's recollections tell much of what happened during his fifty years of work. At the age of sixty-five he reluctantly wrote in his diary: "Hurt my back and turned the farm to Whit." He was not idle thereafter, and continued to do a share of the farm labor with Whit and Whit's son Lawrence, and to keep up his diary. He also started his memoir.

Sally too continued to do her part; at one point, she entered in her husband's diary: "So far this Summer I, Sally, have put 11 qts. peas, 15 qt. bags stringbeans, 8 pts. asparagus and 30 qt. bags sweet corn and 3 pt. raspberries into the freezer. I have canned 16 pt. pear preserves, 18 pts. pickle pears and 21 qts. Tomatoes. Jellies I have made 16 glasses black raspberry, 30 glasses of red raspberry jam, 20 glasses blackberry and 8 glasses of gooseberry jam and so far I have made 10 glasses apple jelly and expect to make more."

Whit and the grandchildren gave them a surprise party for their fiftieth anniversary in 1971. But they were aging. On December 16, 1974, John Lawrence wrote: "I deeded the farm over to Whit today." He fretted over Sally's worsening illnesses and longer stays in Westerly Hospital. On April 7, 1979, she died there. He found the grief hard to overcome, doubly so because of her loyalty to him and devotion to the farm. John Lawrence Davis's days ended on July 2, 1989, at the age of ninety, but not before his memoir was completed and published in a typescript edition, in 1986. (His sister, Marcia, died a few months later, after a last encounter with John Lawrence in a nursing home.)

With his death, the farm entered a new phase. In 1990, Whit and his son Lawrence arranged to have the state of Connecticut buy development rights — to protect the farm permanently from development — and to sell forty-eight acres to be attached to the Barn Island preserve. The purpose was to avoid inheritance taxes and to save the land. But both Whit and Larry bristled with resentment at their perceived loss of freedom. Larry was quoted as saying: "Whose fault is it that the King of England granted this land to us? How many times do we have to buy it back?"

The Davises decided in 2001 to protect the old house and the nearby farm buildings by creating a museum — one, certainly, with uniquely rich contents. The wills of successive generations list a few of the objects to be passed on to those who inherited the homestead. John Jeremiah Davis took care to specify "Indian implements, the Cherry Secretary, copper kettle and whalebone cane and whip, it being my desire that these ancient relics shall remain in the Davis family." His sister, Sarah, bequeathed to her family chairs owned by her great-grandfather William Stanton and her grandfather Jeremiah Davis and four portraits of forebears. To her grand-nephew, Whit, she gave her "open face gold watch."

In 2006, a new nonprofit organization, the Stanton-Davis Museum, Inc., became the owner of the "old homsted." With Whit as spokesman, the move stirred favorable press and scholarly attention. But an enormous amount of work faced the new trustees in planning and financing the transition, and as of 2007 they were just getting started. Whit, as ever, continued to farm on a manageable scale, and to serve as an advocate for his now 355-year-old heritage.

In a reflective mood, Whit seemed in an interview to speak for his father and the many Davises before him: "We are kind of proud of our old farm here. Even though it doesn't look too good today . . . It's just something that I wanted to preserve for the town and for the state. It's disappearing so fast. I go out to the country and I see a four-acre field that's being built — three, four houses on it. Nice, flat, fertile land, there it goes. Once it's gone, it's gone. They're not making any more land, and I figure that the land is here for us to use and survive on, not to destroy. So I made up my mind that they aren't going to build here. I kind of like to preserve things as they were."

John Whitman Davis and his son Lawrence Malcolm Davis sign documents deeding the house and five acres of the farm to a nonprofit organization, the Stanton-Davis Homestead Museum, on September 29, 2006.

NOTE ON SOURCES

The history of the Davis Homestead (the Stanton-Davis farm) has been scattered among family traditions, genealogies of varying age and trustworthiness, and untapped local and state records. This introduction is an attempt to draw with care on these sources and others to present a brief preliminary narrative of the farm's 355 years of existence.

We relied first on the land, probate, mortality, and assessment records of the Town of Stonington, held at the Stonington Historical Society's Richard W. Woolworth Library and at the Stonington Town Hall. In addition, the records of Pequot Plantation, in the New London City Hall (volume 1C, 21), document the 1652 grant to Thomas Stanton that created the farm. The 1937 Historic American Buildings Survey photographs and drawings are listed under "Robert Stanton House," on a Library of Congress web site, lcweb2.loc.gov. See also the nomination form for the National Register of Historic Places (1979), available from the Stanton-Davis Museum.

There is further information about the Stantons and their land transactions in J. Hammond Trumbull and Charles J. Hoadly, eds., *The Public Records of the Colony of Connecticut* (15 volumes, Hartford, 1850-1890); www.colonialct.uconn.edu. We also used Frances M. Caulkins's classic *History of New London, Connecticut* (1852); Clarence Winthrop Bowen's *The Boundary Disputes of Connecticut* (Boston, 1882); and, locally, Williams Haynes, *Stonington Chronology . . . 1649-1949* (Stonington, 1949); and Richard Anson Wheeler, *History of the Town of Stonington, Connecticut* (New London, Connecticut, 1900).   Andrew McFarland Davis's "The Emissions of the Neighboring Governments: Connecticut," in *Currency and Banking in the Province of the Massachusetts Bay* (New York, 1901) helped decipher the costs of land transactions.

On ecology and farming, we used, among other sources, Rudy J. Favretti, *Highlights of Connecticut Agriculture* (1976); Lyman Carrier, *The Beginnings of Agriculture in America* (New York, 1923); Glenn D. Dreyer and William A. Niering, eds., *Tidal Marshes of Long Island Sound: Ecology, History, and Restoration* (Connecticut College Arboretum, Bulletin No. 34, December 1995); Albert Laverne Olson, *Agricultural Economy and the Population in Eighteenth-Century Connecticut* (New Haven, 1935); and David C. Hsiung, "Food, Fuel, and the New England Environment in the War for Independence, 1775-1776," www.uga.edu/colonialseminar/Hsiung%20Essay.pdf.

On the Stantons and slavery: Barbara W. Brown and James M. Rose, *Black Roots in Southeastern Connecticut, 1650-1900* (1980, 2001); Nancy Steenburg and Elizabeth Kading, "The Venture Adventure," *Wrack Lines* (publication of the Connecticut Sea Grant program), 6 (Spring/Summer 2006), 7-10, and of course Venture Smith's *A Narrative of the Life and Adventures of Venture a Native of Africa* (New London, 1798; recently reissued by the New London County Historical Society).

In family history and genealogy, we employed (with caution) William A. Stanton, *A Record, Genealogical, Biographical, Statistical, of Thomas Stanton, of Connecticut, and His Descendants, 1635-1891* (Albany, N.Y., 1891); John D. Baldwin, *Thomas Stanton of Stonington, Conn.: An Incomplete Record of His Descendants* (Worcester, Mass., 1882), and Bernard John Stanton's valuable introduction and transcription of the "Last Will and Testament of Thomas Stanton, Senior, October 24, 1677," March 4, 1984; copy in the Woolworth Library. See also his summary of the farm's history in *The Thomas Stanton Society Newsletter* (No. 23, 2004).

The Davis family's version of the farm's history is summarized in Sarah M. Davis, "History of an Old Connecticut Homestead," *American Monthly Magazine* (Daughters of the American Revolution, August 1912, 45-47). Family history is chronicled in Albert H. Davis, *History of the Davis Family . . .* (New York, 1888); J.H. Beers & Co., *Genealogical and Biographical Record of New London County, Conn.* (2 vols., Chicago, 1905); also John Lawrence Davis, "Farm Diary 1914-1984," typescript, available in the Woolworth Library; "A Sad Death" [Alphonso Davis], *Westerly* (R.I.) *Sun.* May 10, 1908; Sarah Shaw Davis, obituary, *Westerly Sun,* April 8, 1979; John Lawrence Davis, obituary, *The Day* (New London), July 5, 1989; Joe Wojtas, "A Yankee Farmer Makes a Deal—Reluctantly," *The Day,* December 12, 1990. John W. Davis interview is in Kenneth W. Simon documentary, "Working the Land," (2007), www. workingtheland.com/interview-davis.htm. John W. Davis kindly supplied an audio tape recalling his aunt, Marcia Davis Gabrielsen, John Lawrence Davis's sister.

Overleaf: John Lawrence Davis and the pony his Uncle John Jeremiah bought for him when he was three, which dates this picture about 1902. The boy named his horse Jack Farmer and at first rode him bareback because there was no saddle small enough. Davis got a nickel daily from his uncle for rounding up the cows, and the pony became expert at the task. This was the first of Davis's saddle horses. He writes that he always had one. This photograph is one of the few datable early pictures of the homestead. Note the big tree on the south façade, and the fences, which disappeared by the time the Historic American Buildings Survey came to the farm in 1937.

THE DAVIS HOMESTEAD

CHAPTER 1

HISTORY OF THE FARM
(BEGUN IN JUNE 1966)

As I badly strained myself and will be inactive for some time, I decided to write a history of the farm, which I hope will be of interest to someone sometime.

The Davis Homestead, which is the oldest house in the town of Stonington, Connecticut, was built in 1680 by Thomas Stanton, the first Indian interpreter in the area. It was purchased by the Davis family in 1772 from Robert Stanton, grandson of Thomas. It consisted of a large kitchen and hall with a bedroom and large living room (21 x 21 feet) on the first floor. The second floor contained three small bedrooms and one large one the size of the living room below it. The large bedroom is where the first school in the district was held. When the ceiling over the living room had to be replaced, about 1930, many things the school children had lost in the floorboards were found. We found some pieces of homespun cloth, a two-tined fork with bone handle, a leather thimble, arrowheads, an inkwell made of horn, a snuff box, small engraved penknife, the sole from a small child's shoe, and a potato gun.

I was very interested in the potato gun as my uncle had made them for me when I was a small boy. He used the quill of a goose feather for the barrel of the gun by cutting off both ends of the quill. This left a hollow tube. Then he would slice a piece of potato about one-quarter inch in thickness. The wider end of the quill was pushed through the slice, leaving a piece of potato in the quill. He whittled out a stick to just fit in the quill and would push the potato to the other end of the quill, but not quite out. Then he would push the quill through the potato again and the gun was loaded. Push the second piece with the stick and air will build up in the quill. When enough pressure has been obtained, the first piece will pop out and go twenty feet or more. The second piece then becomes the bullet and so on. The one we found was made from a hollow reed and in perfect condition.

There were four fireplaces, two on each floor. One small room upstairs with a fireplace was known as the "Birth Room" because of its small size and it could be heated easily.

The original stone chimney was torn down in 1754 and replaced with brick. The kitchen fireplace and the foundation were still in good condition, so they were left alone, but a new addition was added to the east end of the house with two rooms downstairs and two more upstairs. Also two more fireplaces were added.

There are three "Christian" doors in the house (with a cross formed in the upper part of the panel) one of which is the front entry door. It still has its bronze knocker and butterfly hinges as of 300 years ago. The design of the paneling in the old part of the house is different from that in the new wing. The downstairs two front rooms have folding shutters at the windows and are paneled. Many of the doors have the old "L" and "H" hinges on them and are the original ones. On each end of the house are the original three-foot shingles laid twelve inches to the weather. They are still in good condition. The kitchen fireplace is fifty-seven inches high, seven feet seven inches long and two and a half feet from the backside to the hearth stone in front. The "Dutch oven" is over three feet deep. There is a small smoke hole through the side of the oven that goes high up into the fireplace. Uncle used to tell me how his mother would make pies, pots of beans, bread, biscuits, etc., and after the hot coals had been removed, she would fill it full of things to bake. Cooked in that brick oven, with just a tinge of smoke, how good it used to taste. Even today, there is a better flavor to food baked in the oven of a wood stove rather than by gas or electricity. Far and away, much, much better.

On winter evenings Uncle, Father and Auntie would sit by the fireplace with their father and mother. Grandfather would shell corn by hand to be taken to the mill to be made into johnnycake meal, while the children would pop corn, eat chestnuts, and roast apples. (What a pity that the American chestnut is no more. A blight, brought in from Europe in 1916, killed them all off.) They would partly core the apples, put a bit of sugar in the hole and place them near the coals. When they were done on one side, they would turn them over and do the other side.

My uncle slept in a trundle bed when he was a baby. About 8:30 his father would say, "To bed." He would cover the coals deeply with ashes to hold the coals until morning, when he would uncover them, place on fine kindling and with the bellows start the fire for the day. Before going to bed on cold nights (and winter nights were always cold), he would fill the warming pan with coals and hot ashes and push it around in the beds until the blankets were thoroughly warmed. Sometimes a severe storm would be in progress and Uncle would lie there and listen to the wind howl and the hail beat against the window pane, glad that he was snug in bed. Other times, there would be snow on the windowsill in the morning, where it had sifted in during the night. Sally, my wife, and I never had a fire in our bedroom until after our son, John W., was born and then only because of the baby.

During the administration of F.D. Roosevelt, and as part of the W.P.A. project, the Historic American Buildings Survey came here in 1937 and drew out every room for size and paneling. These drawings are on file at the Library of Congress, Washington, D.C., under the title "Connecticut 1126, Robert Stanton House." I was very glad to see these men as they were experts in their field and I obtained a lot of information from them.

In 1949, we held Open House here in celebration of the three-hundredth anniversary of the founding of the Town of Stonington. Many who went through the house (754 in number), asked about the two heavy beams across the ceiling of the large downstairs living room called "summer trees." Summer trees is not the name they should be called but rather "sumpter beams." In the old days, the pack mule was called the "sumpter mule." He carried the load and as these beams carry the load of the ceiling and the floor above, they are known as sumpter beams.

In 1930, a man named Horace Barber was called in to paint and paper the front hall. He did a wonderful job and being a very thorough man he took off three layers of paint. This brought him down to the original colors. He mixed shades of blue and ivory to match, so now the hall is back to the original colors and looks beautiful.

The banister rail, with three styles of hand carvings, was brought over from England, as was the corner cupboard in the East Parlor with its sunburst effects, when the house was built.

I was born December 3, 1898, and having lost my parents in 1908, I was brought up by my uncle, John J. Davis. He was a good, hard-working man and taught me to drive a team, plow, mow, etc., all things I should know about running a farm. He told me all the things his father had told him when he was a boy. We have owned this farm since 1772 and leased it for ten years prior to that.

In 1814, when the British fleet was off the Stonington coast, John Davis thought they couldn't be stopped, so he had a man stationed at Osbrook Point as lookout. The oxen and livestock were in the barnyard, the oxen yoked and the horses harnessed. The wagons were loaded by the door with all the household goods that could be piled on them; beds, dishes, etc., as he expected the British to come up the Pawcatuck River from Stonington to raid and plunder. He had no hope of saving the farm buildings. His lookout on the point could warn him in time to drive the stock away from the river, up into the wilderness of North Stonington, and hide them in the woods. As the British didn't come, he didn't have to leave the farm. It was a very trying three days. My uncle's grandfather was six years of age at that time but remembered the details very well, as all the excitement made a lasting impression on him.

My uncle told me about the piece of land here at the farm known as the Continental. This is a large marsh and during the Revolutionary War our folks were asked to give money to the Continental Army. Not having much to spare, they mowed this piece of marsh for hay. They sold it to the farmers away from the river and gave the money derived from it to the Continentals. The hay sold readily because it was salt, which was relished by the stock inland. Some was carted directly to the army for their horses. This was done every year of the war and so this marsh is still called the Continental, because it had been reserved for the army during the war.

My uncle was born in 1854 and he told me stories about his boyhood that were very interesting. The money from the farm was derived mostly from cattle and sheep. There were about a dozen or more cows that were milked mostly in the warm months. They had grass to eat which took the place of grain, somewhat, as a great deal of grain would be required to make milk in the winter months and there were no grain stores in those days. The milk was made into cheese and butter. The whey and skimmed milk was fed to the calves and pigs. The butter and cheese went to the grocery store in Stonington to be traded for molasses, sugar, tea, coffee, things that were not produced on the farm. Much of the cheese found its way onto the whalers when they were outfitted in Stonington Harbor.

The farm supplied practically all the essentials required for food and, I am proud to say, it still does, although more is purchased from a store now than in his day. One staple I have had many, many times is mush and milk. The mush is made of johnnycake meal, hot water and a little salt. Instead of frying in a skillet on the stove, it is boiled. It is really cornmeal, as oatmeal is made from oats.

There used to be a man with a horse and a very long wagon with high sides, from which hung long ladders, stepladders, pails, pitchforks, wooden ladles, bowls, spoons, ax handles — you name it, he had it. He had a regular route he traveled and would spend the night at certain places along the way. He and his horse would be "put up" and fed. One place he always stayed was here at the farm. Uncle was about 10 or 11 at the time. One night, when they were sitting down to supper, they heard a team pass by the house and go toward the barn. "John," said his father, "you take the lantern and go help him put his horse in the barn and feed it." Uncle did as he was told. When they had finished with the horse and coming back to the house, the peddler asked my uncle what they were having for supper. Uncle said, "Mush and milk." "Well," said the peddler, "mush and milk is very nourishing no doubt, but as far as filling you up is concerned, you might as well open your mouth and let the moon shine down your throat." Uncle laughed about that all his life.

The sheep were kept down at Osbrook Point all winter and fed from haystacks. A pail of corn was fed them each day for nourishment and to keep them around as they would stay close to their feeding place. Once after a blizzard the sheep couldn't be found, although the point was searched thoroughly. The next day the search was continued and someone noticed steam rising from a huge drift beside a high wall. Upon examining the drift, it was discovered that the sheep had made a runway next to the wall and although they were completely covered with snow, not one was lost or sick.

The sheep stayed out all winter and were brought back to the barn in April to lamb. They were kept there until the lambs were strong enough to go to pasture. After shearing, about seventy-five sheep and their lambs were turned out to pasture again. As early as when I was a small boy, I remember going down to the point and driving a bunch of sheep into a holding pen (part of which is still standing) and catching lambs for market. We would bring up about eight or ten in the express wagon at a time. They were tied by three legs, one hind leg between both forelegs and one hind leg left loose. This was so they could be lifted without hurting them with the rope they were tied with. Upon arrival at the barn, they would be turned into some good afterfeed (grass that grows back after being mowed) to fatten. They were induced to eat grain also, which was cornmeal. Uncle used to mark them with a red powder he mixed up, making one stripe across the lamb's back. Two stripes for those brought up ten days later and three stripes for those brought up ten days after that.

Money was very scarce in my uncle's boyhood days and one means of raising some was by setting snares and stone deadfalls for rabbits, quail, partridge, and squirrels. All the neighborhood boys set traps also and they would carry their catch to school. At lunch time, they would eat hurriedly and then rush to Westerly to sell their game to a store that would send it to New York. They received 10 cents for a rabbit, 15 cents for a partridge and 5 cents for one quail or squirrel. They not only made it back to school by one o'clock, but were highly elated that they could make so much money.

When I was six years old, my father took me to the woods and set me a stone trap. He told me that his grandfather set the stone for his father, who set it for him and he said for me to set it for my son and to continue it on. This has been done by all of us.

I always liked the woods and to set traps. Between 1933 and 1934, I caught sixty-two muskrats and had a fur coat made for my wife, Sally, from the skins. My uncle showed me how to braid a snare made from the hair plucked from the tail of a horse and to make a hedge in the woods and set the snare.

The things my father and uncle enjoyed besides hunting and trapping were swimming, driving and riding horses, skating with bonfires on the ice, hanging May baskets, etc. One thing that was really amusing to Uncle, was, as he termed it, "yipping cats." After his mother skimmed the milk, the cream of which was made into butter, she would fill a pan full for several very large wild barn cats that would come and drink from the pan. Uncle always liked to frighten them and see them run for the brush and weeds around the barn. The way he encouraged them to excessive speed was to throw egg-sized stones at them with more or less accuracy. One night he hid behind the corner of the house armed with a plentiful supply of ammunition. His mother filled the pan and returned to the house. Uncle peered around the corner with one eye and watched as five or six cats came warily up to the pan. They didn't see anyone, but were highly suspicious. They would put their heads in the pan, take a few laps, then raise their heads and look fearfully around. Just as they all lowered their heads again, Uncle jumped out from his hiding place and let drive a rock. By dint of long practice and extra good luck, the stone landed squarely in the middle of the pan splashing the cats with milk and overturning the pan with a loud BANG. Every cat went immediately three feet high, turned while in the air and began to run desperately for their lives before their feet even touched the ground. Uncle let out a couple of "yips" which were entirely wasted, as the cats had already done their best. I have heard Uncle tell this story many times and he always laughed so heartily he would almost fall out of the chair.

Before the gasoline engine and circular saw came into general use, all wood for the fireplace had to be bucksawed or chopped with an ax. One method of bringing the wood home to the woodpile was to cut down a tree, trim off the branches with an ax, and with a pair of oxen drag the resulting log across the frozen ground or snow to the woodpile by the house. Here it was sawed or cut into suitable lengths for the fireplace. One day, when Uncle was in his late teens or early twenties, he was bringing such a log out the woods along a narrow path. The oxen were being driven by a boy named John O'Connell. Uncle was standing close to a curve in the path directing the job, when the log came to the corner it turned of course, but the back end slid across the path and before Uncle could jump out of the way, it struck his legs and broke his left leg completely between the knee and ankle. He was helpless. John stopped the oxen and ran to the farm for help.

My father hitched up a horse and buggy and went to the woods and brought Uncle home. A doctor came and set the broken bones and put the leg in a cast. Weeks later when the cast was removed, it was found to have been set crooked and so the doctor broke and reset it. After it began to knit, a box was made long enough to admit the length of his leg through a hole in one end. The box was filled in some way with steam, which was supposed to soften the bone and induce and hasten healing. Needless to say, he suffered terribly and that leg was always shrunken below the knee and was shorter than the other. I have seen the box which was used.

One day, I was talking with one of my milk customers I had had for several years. He was a very old man named O'Connell. He had two grown sons and a daughter. He began asking me about the farm and seemed very familiar with the locations of different fields. I was surprised and asked how he knew so much about it. "Why," said he, "I was the boy who was with your uncle when he broke his leg in the woods." He then told me all about it. One of his jobs before he went to the Lower Pawcatuck School every morning was to take a pail of corn and feed the sheep down at Osbrook Point. Then he came back and walked another mile to school. He didn't seem to think much about the distance. It was just a chore; everybody walked and worked in those days and thought nothing of it.

The first stove came into this house about 1871. It was a kitchen or cookstove and was very heavy. It had four or six lids on the top for frying and boiling and an oven for baking. Uncle's mother didn't like it for a long time as she preferred to cook in the fireplace. The fireplace is so large that the stove was set inside it and somewhere around the house is a faded picture of the stove set-up.

I have said that the best revenue from the farm was milk made into cheese and sold in Stonington for the whaling ships. When the whaling industry stopped, the cheese business also stopped. Then they had to look for another market for their milk. Fortunately for them, the summer resort at Watch Hill, Rhode Island, began to boom. Everything such as milk, cream

The kitchen fireplace is 7 feet 7 inches wide. The Dutch Oven is at the left. Below, the cookstove that was set into the fireplace about 1871. (Top photograph: Brown Brothers)

and vegetables became in great demand. Transportation was a problem not easily solved; it had to be by boat or horse. My father and Uncle went to the Ocean House, one of the larger hotels, to see if they wanted milk. The answer was yes, all they could get.

Father and Uncle increased the herd to eighteen milkers and built a new barn just for the cows. They hired a stall in Horace Burdick's barn in Avondale, Rhode Island, carried the milk across the river in a boat, hitched up the horse, loaded the milk from the boat into the wagon and drove to Watch Hill to the Ocean House. This they kept up for several years. One day a guest at the hotel, having rented a cottage for the summer, inquired of the manager where could he buy milk to be delivered to his rented home. Father was consulted and agreed to deliver it at a retail price. Soon Father had a retail trade, all he could take care of. He used to sell 150 quarts per day in the summer.

Besides the milk, there was a great demand for vegetables, lamb, chicken and eggs. Father then increased the flock to 400 hens and bought eggs and chickens for the trade. Milk was also purchased from the neighbors and set in the cooler to skim when the cream rose to the top. The cream was sold and the skimmed milk went to the pigs. One boar and two sows were kept which would litter a total of ten to fourteen pigs. They were butchered in the fall and sausage, bacon, etc., was sold to the neighbors at retail prices.

My uncle and father worked hard and I mean hard, from three o'clock in the morning until long after dark. The fieldwork had to be done in the daytime, such as haying, hoeing, and vegetable picking. Father, Uncle, a Negro named Ase Carpenter (more about him later), and even myself used to pick and pinfeather forty to fifty chickens every Thursday. They were then packed in ice in a large icebox and, Saturday night, weighed, split, and tagged for the "Hill." Father bought two very large lamps which he hung under the shed and he and Uncle would dress the chickens until after eleven o'clock at night. Up again at three o'clock in the morning when Uncle

would milk fifteen to seventeen cows alone while Father was
bottling milk and cream. A horse was brought to the door, the
wagon was loaded and at 5:30 was driven down to the boat
and so on its way to Watch Hill. I used to go sometimes with
Father and the cooks would treat me to cake and candy. Father
always tried to be at Watch Hill at six o'clock in the morning
so the customers could have fresh milk for their breakfast.
There was no electric refrigeration then, but the ice wagons
did a rushing business. Everyone was working hard and
making enough money to pay their bills. There wasn't an
income tax and the taxes on the farm were less than $20 for
the year. Today, in 1971, the farm is taxed for $1,100.

There were other milkmen on the Hill besides us. I
remember Palmer Chapman who also kept a grocery store,
the two Breen brothers, George Champlin and Phil Rexroth,
who drove a big wagon with a team and also a one-horse wagon,
every day from Ashaway, Rhode Island, loaded with eggs,
chickens and vegetables, but no milk. The price of milk retailed
at Watch Hill up to 1908 for 8 cents per quart. This was about
3 cents more than the year-round price in Westerly. We had
to maintain our herd of cows all winter, with nothing coming
in, so the profit wasn't very much. In the winter we sold eggs,
geese in the holiday season, as well as johnnycake meal. Every
ten days or so, Uncle and I would carry eight bushels of shelled
corn to the grist mill, and would pick up the previous week's
corn all ground into meal. We would then take it to the grocery
store where it would be applied to our account. The corn meal
would just about pay for our groceries.

After 1908, and the death of Father, it was difficult for
Uncle to manage the farm alone. He hired some help and did
the best he could until I was old enough to run the farm. I was
married on June 4, 1921, and have been on the farm ever
since. In 1964, I turned the management over to my son, Whit,
for I felt I was getting too old to run it any longer.

Farming is a good business and if you work the land, it
will always keep you. Remember that. Keep out of debt. If you
can't pay for a thing when you buy it, you can't pay for it

later, either. Work your farm with good horses, no matter what.

I mentioned before a Negro who worked here named Ase Carpenter. He had a brother named Bill who worked for my cousin, Dan Davis, on the next farm. Ase was a very hard-working man and prided himself on being able to out-work any man he ever saw. He could and did. He could mow better with a scythe than with a lawn mower; his scythe would practically shave the ground. He taught me how to do it, too. His movements were easy and graceful. I never saw him drive a horse, but he could make oxen do tricks, except for Monday mornings when he would be nursing a big head from his usual weekend drunk. He was the greatest humorist that there ever was. I don't know where he came from but he used to go to school with Father, Uncle, and the neighborhood boys, so he must have always lived around here. He had a wife and stepdaughter. Father and Uncle built a three-room house for them over in the back lot, where they lived in perfect contentment. Sade, his wife, worked for the neighbors doing washing, cleaning, and cooking and so did her daughter Edith. Edith married a George Simonds. They would go off for a while, but would always come home to "Ma."

My mother employed Sade for washing clothes and ironing. She asked Sade (who had no screens on the doors or windows) what they did about the mosquitoes at night. "Oh, they don't bother much," she replied. "We get a pail of cow manure and fill a large iron pot with it. Then we light it at night and place it in the open doorway. It makes a good smudge and we can forget about the 'skeeters'." Mother spoke to Father about it and he bought some screens. They hadn't even thought about it until Mother put the idea in their heads.

Ase would tell a joke on himself and laugh heartily over it. He was a great mimic and could clown about or imitate almost anyone, and while working in the fields, he would have us laughing. He used to refer to one of his thumbs (which had been broken one day while catching a hog) as his "mud-turtle" thumb. The joint had enlarged in healing, so it was twice the size it should be and being black, he said, it looked like the head of a mud-turtle.

Now cider was, and is still, an important item on the farm. It has no overhead at all. The best apples were carefully picked and stored for winter. The surplus apples were made into cider. Cider was to New England what moonshine was to Kentucky: "The Drink." Father used to have, including vinegar, twelve or more barrels in the cellar all the time. One of these barrels was filled with sugar, raisins, etc., and carefully watched. The bung was driven in just tight enough to keep the proper pressure to ensure the cider from getting flat. This barrel was for home use and guests and was known as the "Minister's Barrel," because when the minister called he, as honored guest, was entitled to the best cider. I don't know whether the ministers drank much or any of it, although I know of one who did and I believe others did too. It was a good beverage, anyway.

Now the cider was of varying degrees of potency. Ase had his particular names for three of the barrels. One was "Old Hat." That barrel was newly made and was "soft" and felt pretty good. Another was called "Red Eyes." That was better, but all it did was make your eyes red and run water. The third was called "Tanglefoot." That was two years old and would mix your feet up so you couldn't walk.

Ase would figure up with Father what he had used during the week, such as pork from the barrel to make chowder or cook with beans, potatoes, johnnycake meal, eggs, sausages, and whatever else we had for sale that he might need. One thing was always included, and that, you might guess, was a gallon of cider to last over Sunday. Ase's brother Bill and wife, George Simonds, and their friends would visit him on Sunday afternoon and what could be better than to treat them to some good cider. Sometimes more friends would call than he had planned on, so he just sent for more cider.

Now my mother was quite a churchgoer and did not approve of Father selling cider on Sunday. She spoke to Father about it, and then he spoke to Ase about it. Ase was dejected for a moment only, then he brightened up and said, "Oh, that's all right, I'll get two gallons on Saturday night, then if I have a lot of company, I will have enough. If I don't have too many, I will just drink that much more myself." And that was the way it was. If I remember correctly, Mother's eyes had a slight twinkle when Father told her how Ase had solved the problem.

One night when Ase was getting his two gallons of cider, he specified what he wanted. One gallon of Red Eye and one gallon of Tanglefoot. "Put the Red Eye in the glass jug and the Tanglefoot in the crock jug," he said, "so I will know which is which. I got some company coming tomorrow and I want to give them a good time." "Look Al," he said to Father, holding his face toward the light which shone in from the open cellar doorway, "I have worked so hard today that I am black in the face. Don't you think I should have a glass of cider?" Father looked at him as if seeing him for the first time and exclaimed, "Ase, you have worked hard and you are black in the face, I think you should have two glasses of cider." So Ase got his free drinks and they both laughed together as they left the cellar.

When Ase came to work Monday morning, father asked him how he made out with the cider and his company. "Well," said Ase with a big laugh, "we drank up the Red Eye and when that was gone he wanted more. I brought the Tanglefoot out of the bedroom and set the jug on the table. He already had his arms resting on the table and after each glass of Tanglefoot, he leaned on them more heavily. Then his head began to sag lower and lower till it rested on the table, too. I couldn't wake him up until along about midnight. He sure had a good time."

I have already mentioned that the best apples were picked for winter use and the others were used for cider. One day Uncle and Ase were picking apples over in the west orchard, which is near the Negro cabin. Uncle was on the ground and Ase high in the tree picking apples into a pail which he lowered to Uncle by means of a long rope, to empty for him. Uncle was busy with the apples when he heard someone on the other side of the wall in the direction of Ase's house. He turned to see Ase's mother-in-law standing there. She thinking Uncle was alone and apparently wishing to talk to somebody about what was on her mind, began to unburden herself to Uncle. Ase was the subject, the whole subject, and nothing but the subject. Everything about him was bad or worse. One of her remarks was, "When Sade married him, I told her if she burned badly, she would have to sit on the blister." More remarks and more talk. Finally Uncle, who was enjoying himself thoroughly, thought he would inform her occupant. Looking up at the tree he called out, "Come, Ase, I think you can pick a few more big ones without moving the ladder." The woman looked up and saw Ase sitting there motionless and taking in every word. With a look of consternation on her face, she hurried back to the house. "There, Ase," said Uncle, "now you know what people think of you." "Huh," replied Ase, "she is only a mother-in-law." Thus, he lightly brushed it off.

While on the subject of apples, I want to say that great grandfather was a good orchardist. He had a piece of ground which is still called the nursery. Here, he planted apple seed and grafted the seedlings. All the apple orchards in Lower Pawcatuck came from his nursery. There must have been seven hundred trees or more. They were set on different farms from the Pawcatuck River to Wequetequock. I think this is a very conservative estimation. He had many varieties including Prentice russet, sweet russet, and Chesebrough russet, Baker's sweeting, August sweeting, golden sweeting, spicing, Denison redding, Hubbard nonesuch, Rhode Island greening, summer greening, Baldwin, pippin, sheepnose or gillyflower, snow, strawberry, belleflower and Peck's pleasant. All of these apples I have saved by grafting seedlings from the old trees and I now have a fine orchard just as Grandfather had. These hard apples make far better cider than the "soft" or MacIntosh variety.

In 1880, Uncle brought a cider mill from Norwich, Connecticut. It was brought on a boat down the Thames River to New London, then along the coast and up the Pawcatuck

River to the dock where it was unloaded and brought up to the farm by oxen. It was set up and cider was made from it for ten or fifteen years; then it was abandoned for the custom cider mill, which was run by water power or a gasoline engine. The price then for making it was only 2 cents per gallon or about $1 per barrel. A barrel could be pressed out in twenty minutes, so it was much better than the hand mill.

As the year 1900 came along, the sheep business at Osbrook Point became a headache. Dogs became numerous and the damage was great. Osbrook Point was sold in 1902 to a Mr. Jacob Lett of New York City, whose intentions were to build a house there. He only lived a few months after that and the property was again sold, this time to a Mr. Fairweather of Westerly, who also only lived a few months. It was then purchased by a Miss Sullivan of the Watch Hill Road for the purpose of preserving its natural beauty, as there was a beautiful grove of majestic oak trees. She told my folks to use it as their own property, but to keep campers out and to watch out for fires. This they gladly agreed to. My folks, in selling it, had thought it would become a small summer resort, where they could sell their farm products without going all the way to Watch Hill.

As I said, the dog damage was serious, to the extent that the flock was reduced to about twenty head. They were kept around the barn except for the summer months. I have seen my father stop still in the kitchen and listen intently, then go outdoors and listen again. He could hear dogs barking at the point, and with that, would grab his double-barreled twelve-gauge shotgun, run to the barn, saddle Jim (his own black horse), and ride like mad for the Point. Jim was the fastest horse he had, but Father had to go on foot after he arrived there, as Jim was gunshy and Father couldn't fire from his back. Sometimes we could hear the gun fired and then some yelping, then the dogs were wounded. Other times we heard the gun and no yelping, then the dogs were dead. Finally, the flock was reduced to twelve or fifteen head and they were kept around the barn all year round. After I was married and began to run the farm, I worked the flock up to fifty-four head and kept them at the Point six or seven months of the year. Then Miss Sullivan died and the Point was sold again so we had to stop using the land. We now have twelve or fifteen sheep around and they have to be put in the barn at night because of the dogs.

From early 1850 to 1890, Osbrook Point was a favorite picnic area. On the river side, still standing today, is the remainder of a dock that I remember as having spiles that extended out into the water to accommodate large boats and barges. There was a large dance hall in the grove, swings for the children and places for clambakes and open fires. The trees were so tall, they provided a shade so that no underbrush existed at all. The Westerly tugboat would bring church picnics by towing a barge large enough to hold the entire crowd. The barge would tie up to the wharf and the tugboat would call for them to get them back home before dark. What a time! Baseball, swings, chowder, and walks through the woods. All of this brought some revenue into the pockets of my uncle and father. They rented the grounds, washed the dishes, hung the swings, kept the dance hall clean, set out the tables and chairs and in general provided whatever was needed.

Uncle's father must have done so also, as my Aunt Sarah M. Davis (my father's sister), who helped bring my sister Marcia and me up, used to tell about the horse buggies going through the lots on the way to the picnic. There were three gates that had to be opened and closed both coming and going. Uncle, Father and Aunt Sarah (all children at the time) each tended a gate for the convenience of the drivers of the buggies. The charge for opening a gate was one penny. Auntie used to laugh about it: as one team was followed by another, she would quickly close the gate, then politely open it again and charge the penny fee. Now not all the picnics were church affairs, by a long shot.

Boxing in those days was outlawed. Nevertheless, there was a ring of standards of 4-by-4-inch pieces of wood about two and one-half or three feet high with a hole at the top end through which a rope was passed joining them all together making a good sized ring. This could be gathered up instantly and put away quickly or easily set up again. I have seen the ring and feel sure it wasn't made just to be looked at.

When Miss Sullivan purchased the Point, she had the dance hall removed and someone built a house with the lumber. I believe the name of the man was Wilbur and the house he built is on Mystic Avenue in Lower Pawcatuck.

Uncle kept a few goats with the sheep on Osbrook Point and the men at the picnic would have great sport with the billy goat. He was a large goat and had a very long beard. The boys would offer him a large mug of beer, which the goat greatly relished. They would get the goat so drunk that foam would completely drench his beard. Then they would laugh and tease him and he couldn't do more than bob his head and fall down. He was a great attraction and always in demand.

Along about 1900, Angora hair or wool was in great demand for coats. Angora coats were very fashionable and all the rage. You were really "somebody" if you had such a coat, whether you had another dollar or not. Already having a small flock of female goats, Uncle thought he might be able to entice a few more nickels into the Davis cash drawer if he could get one of these Angora billys and mate him with his present flock of goats. The resulting offspring would be half Angora and the hair would bring top price. With this in mind, he began to inquire around as to where he could obtain such an animal.

Finally, he heard of one, so hitching up his horse he drove to a nearby farm and inquired if there was a billy for sale. The man said, "Yes," he had a nice one for sale. Uncle asked to see him and was taken to the barn. Uncle went in but didn't see any goat. "Oh," said the man in an easy offhand kind of way, "I keep him in the box stall over there." He opened the door and although there were no windows in the place, he could see a beautiful Angora billy very plainly. Uncle inquired if he was a good breeder and the asking price. The owner said he was a sure breeder and named a seemingly ridiculously low price. Uncle said he would take him, which he did the next day. Upon arriving home, he turned the billy out with the other goats. They seemed to get along fine and when he left them, the billy was quietly feeding. Uncle felt quite elated at having bought such a fine animal for such a low price.

The next day, he went to the goat pasture to feed the flock and discovered the billy missing. Quite upset and worried, Uncle began to search for him. He looked over the entire pasture and then began to search outside of it. Sure enough there was the billy in a nice mowing lot, calmly feeding on the best grasses. Uncle drove him back into the goat pasture with the other goats but couldn't find where he had gotten out.

Everything seemed all right that night, but the next morning the billy was out again. Same place, over the stone wall, in the mowing lot. This time Uncle drove him into the barn and closed the door. He went to the house to get Ase, a narrow barrel stave, some pieces of leather from harness reins, and a large bit for boring wood. These, he and Ase carried back to the barn. Ase caught the goat and held him squarely on his feet while Uncle measured him for the hobble. Uncle held the barrel stave up against the goat's legs just above the ankles on the left side. With his jackknife, he scratched a mark on the board opposite each leg. He then bored a hole large enough to admit the leather rein and pushed an end of the rein through the hole around the goat's leg and brought it back through the same hole, making a loop with both ends on the same side of the board. He then, with the point of his jackknife, pushed a slit through the ends of the leather and inserted a wooden key which he made with a notch in the middle to hold it from slipping out. He did the same thing with the other leg. When they finished, the goat had to walk with both legs on the left side at the same time. This didn't hurt him any and he could get around and feed, but not being able to put both front legs forward at the same time, he couldn't jump. (I have hobbled many jumping sheep with this device and it always worked.)

Uncle turned the flock out of the barn and the billy fought the stick a few steps, then went quietly to feeding. "There," said Uncle, "I guess that will hold you for a while." And it did, for just three days and he was out again, over the wall and in the mowing lot. Muttering something to himself, Uncle drove the goat back into the barn, got Ase, more wood and leather and put a similar hobble on the other side. Then when the billy walked, he was forced to pace like a horse one side at a time. He soon learned to do this so expertly, that he could beat any other member of the flock across the lot. This lasted about ten days, then he was out again and into the mowing lot.

About this time in that goat's life, whenever Uncle saw or thought of him, there would appear a deep gleam in Uncle's eyes, but it wasn't one of pride of ownership. Grimly he drove the billy into the barn again, got Ase, and started for the woods. When he returned, he had a green stick about two inches thick and bended easily. Ase caught the goat and Uncle removed the hobble on the right side. He then untied the left front leg and swinging the hobble across to the right front leg, he securely fastened it there. Then he made another hobble of the green stick, fastened one end to the right hind leg, crossed it over the barrel stave to the left foreleg and fastened that leg.

This method seemed to puzzle the goat quite a bit when Uncle let him out of the barn into the lot. He walked as best he could, but he seemed to realize that he was severely handicapped. However, he apparently was going to make the best of it and seemed quite cheerful. Uncle seemed in better humor after viewing his job on the goat. He watched him perform with the cross hobble. He would go a little way, then stumble and catch himself. He kept this up until he could go quite a distance without stumbling. As soon as he ceased to stumble, he began to work for speed. Soon he was able to get around real handy, but he didn't jump out. That is, he didn't jump out for three weeks. Then he was out again and over the wall. This time Uncle went to the woodpile, got a piece of log two feet long and one foot thick. He tied a rope around the middle of the log, drove in some staples to keep the rope from coming out, and tied the other end to the goat's hind legs. Cross-hobbled and with this heavy billet of wood on behind for a drag, the billy was finally subdued and stopped jumping for five weeks. Then he was out again.

This time Uncle brought him over to the house and tied him on an iron bar set firmly in the ground. The rope was about twenty feet long and tied firmly around the goat's neck. The hobbles were removed and he could only go the length of the rope. He was tied on the lower terrace in the front yard. I was cautioned not to go down there or anywhere near the billy, but being four years of age, that was the first place I went. I got too close. The goat ran around behind me. The rope came against my legs and trapped me. Down I went, yelling for all I was worth. Everyone came running to rescue me.

Father and Uncle held a consultation about the goat with the result that Uncle butchered it the next week. He had the horns mounted and the skin tanned and made into a rug which lay on the front hall floor for many years. The hair was long, curly and white and it really made a nice rug. Later, Uncle thought back and remembered the kind of stall the goat was confined in when he purchased him and the fact that it was boarded all the way up to the haymow floor above, without any windows, seemed highly significant.

When the boys in the Davis family reached the age of sixteen, they were trusted to have a gun. When Uncle John reached that age, his father took him to Stonington one day to purchase one. The price was $5 and it was a muzzle loader, with a ramrod, of course. It was light to carry and an accurate shooter. I never saw the gun fired, but Uncle told me how to load it by pouring powder in until when you put the ramrod all the way down and put your first and second fingers together on the end of the muzzle. The ramrod end that protruded came just to the height of the thickness of the two fingers. That was known as two fingers of powder and was used for all normal distance shots. When loading for a greater distance three fingers were used instead of two, making a heavier charge.

Uncle was very fond of his gun and used it many, many times. He told me of the wonderful shots he made with it. One day he made a long distance shot at a squirrel and when he picked it up he was surprised to see another hunter close by, who had seen Uncle make the shot. The hunter, who apparently was well-to-do, asked to see the gun. Uncle let the man take it and he examined it closely. He asked what Uncle had paid for it and when told $5, he said, "You have a better gun than I have and mine cost $25." This, of course, pleased Uncle very much. This was the year 1870, when breech loaders came out. Uncle bought a double barreled shotgun, ten gauge.

All the business and trading for the farm was done in Stonington. The grocery, hardware, and clothing stores were there and they supplied the town. One day, as Uncle's father was passing a neighbor's house on his way to Stonington, the man of the house came out and requested him to do an errand for him. This was the usual procedure, for one neighbor to help another, as you never knew when you might want something yourself. Grandfather was very happy to help him. The man's name was "Uncle Joe" Bryant. He brought out a jug and said he wanted a gallon of rum and he told Grandfather that if he saw any of his friends over there, to give them a drink on him.

Grandfather went on to Stonington, did his trading, and had the jug filled with rum. He put it in his wagon and then drove around visiting. He exchanged news from his end of town for news over there, and everywhere he went he inquired if they knew Uncle Joe Bryant. When a group saw the jug and heard about a free drink, it was surprising how many acquaintances Uncle Joe had. Grandfather did as he was requested and then started home. At Bryant's house, Uncle Joe came out to meet him. He eyed the jug with much anticipation and pleasure. "Did you see any of my friends over there?" he asked, "Sure did," replied Grandfather and handed Joe the jug. Joe hefted it and it seemed awfully light. He swished what was left of the rum around in the jug and said mornfully, "Gee, I didn't know I had so many friends."

A painting in the homestead of the Watch Hill, Rhode Island, Lifesaving Station. Walter Davis, a cousin, was captain of this station. Sam Bryant, a neighbor in Pawcatuck, made two paintings of the station, probably in the 1890s.

Uncle Joe had two sons, Joe and Sam. Sam was a naturally born artist. He could paint landscapes that were easily recognized. They were beautiful and we have three of them at the farm, two of Watch Hill Lighthouse Point from one side and one from the other side. He painted these pictures around 1890, I believe. A cousin of ours, Walter Davis, was Captain of Watch Hill Life Saving Station then and around 1904 or 1905. I remember going with Father and Mother to the station to visit the Captain and his wife. Sam's pictures depict things just as they were at that time. While I am on the subject of the Life Saving Station, I want to mention a boat drill that was required and performed by Captain Walt and his crew every week during the summer. They had to take the Life Saving boat out, rowed by six men, capsize, bail out, and row back to the station. This maneuver attracted a large crowd. Pictures were taken, put on post cards, and sold as souvenirs at the Hill for many years.

Uncle John and Joe Bryant were great friends. Uncle would go to visit there evenings. One evening, the subject of clothes came up and was discussed at some length. During the conversation Joe let slip that his father slept with his shoes on. He only took his shoes off once in a while to change his socks. Uncle didn't believe him. Joe said he would prove it. So one night when Uncle Joe said he was very tired and would go to bed, Uncle said he would leave as he didn't want them to stay up for him. Young Joe winked at him and told him to stay for a while. After a few minutes, he tiptoed over to the bedroom door and listened. He came back and told Uncle to wait a few minutes. After a while, he listened again and then he told Uncle to follow him. They carefully went into the bedroom. Joe eased up the covers from the foot of the bed and there was Uncle Joe, fast asleep with his shoes on.

Young Joe had a gun, of course, and claimed it would outshoot the one Uncle had. There was quite a discussion about it and Joe said he would prove it. He would shoot a tallow candle through an inch board 25 feet away. Uncle said he would like to see him do it. Sometime later, Uncle stopped at Joe's and Joe said, "I have my gun all loaded and I'll show you that candle business." He put a board against the wall across the road, placed his gun with the stock against a boulder at the bottom of the wall opposite the board about twenty-five feet away. He then got on his stomach and sighted the gun on the target by placing a block of wood under the end of the barrel. He then tied a string to the trigger and ran the other through the wall to the other side. Uncle asked why all the preparation and Joe said he had such an almighty charge of powder in the old gun, he was afraid to hold it as it might blow up. He went back to the wall, took hold of the string and pulled. There was a mighty explosion, a great cloud of smoke and they could see a hole in the board. Uncle never did see the candle and Joe never tried it again.

I remember when I was four or five years old, Ase Carpenter worked steady here then and he was my hero. Everything he said or did, I tried to do the same. He taught me a number of verses of poetry, some good and some bad. I remember all of them. One I will write down:

Cold, frosty morning
Darkey feelin' good
Ax on his shoulder
For to cut his master's wood
Dry, rusty ash cake
Not a bit of fat
Old Darkey grumbled
Because he ate too much of that.

Another one went:

Way upon a mountain
Slippery as glass
Down came the Devil
Sliding on the ice.

I repeated it after him and then said, "That doesn't rhyme." He looked at me and seeing I knew what would make it rhyme, he grew mockingly serious and with a twinkle in his eye, said, "Look here now, you know as well as I that the top of a mountain is covered with snow and ice all the time. Now on a place like that, what else could he have been sliding on? Of course it was ice." "All right," I said, "then it was ice. But I know better." Then how he would slap his leg and laugh. This greatly complimented me and I always tried to be as much of a man as he.

One day Ase was pitching manure into the ox wagon to be taken to the fields for fertilizer. Now no hard work, and it was all hard work, could be done without the proper amount of cider. Cider took the ache out of your back and kept the work going smoothly. At least, that's the way Ase figured! Therefore, there was a large white pitcher of Ase's favorite beverage on the back wall by the barn. He helped himself to it when he felt thirsty and that was real often. My sister, Marcia, and I were playing around there when he came for a drink. He drank a large cup full, wiped his mouth with the back of his hand and sighed contentedly. I asked what he was drinking and he said, "That is cider, a man's drink." I smelled it and then poured myself a drink. Ase watched intently to see what would happen.

I drank it down and said "Oh" as he had done. Marcia wanted some, so I gave her a cupful. I almost immediately began to feel strange; dizzy and sleepy. I curled up beside the henhouse with Marcia next to me and knew no more until I awakened in the bedroom where Ase had carried us both in answer to mother's call to dinner. Mother was frightened at first until she found out what ailed us and then she gave Ase a good piece of her mind and me the rest of it the next day. That was my first introduction to cider and while I never admired it, I learned to treat it with respect. (Like the fellow who called his cider Firecracker. He said you could take three drinks, but you were no good after the Fourth.)

The parents of John Lawrence Davis: Alphonso Whitman Davis, born in 1861, and Ida May Palmer Davis, in portraits that might be wedding pictures. They both died in 1908. Below, studio portraits of John Lawrence Davis and his sister, Marcia Louise, perhaps about the time he started school at seven.

John Lawrence Davis on the farm as a child with his Uncle John Jeremiah Davis. When his parents died, he was nine and his sister, Marcia, was seven. The children were reared by their uncle, his wife, Elizabeth Hamilton Davis, and his uncle's sister, Sarah. Below, John Lawrence Davis, again wearing a child's smock, feeding geese and hens. He was probably less than four years old.

Young John Lawrence Davis spins a rope. Bill Rovelto, a farm visitor in 1918, taught the young Davis how.

Ase Burnside Carpenter was an African American who grew up around Pawcatuck and lived and worked on the farm early in the 20th century. He taught young Davis many farm skills: swinging a scythe smoothly and chopping wood. Davis describes the teaching this way: "'Real fine, see how old Burns does it,' he would say. 'Now you do it just as old Burns did.'"

Staircase and banister in the homestead, showing the varied designs of the balusters. Family tradition says this elaborate woodwork was imported from England when the house was built by the first Thomas Stanton. The photograph was made by the Historic American Buildings Survey.

Exterior of the Stanton-Davis homestead's front door with "Christian" design, named for the cross in the upper structure. Photograph was taken for Historic American Buildings Survey in 1937.

Front, or south, facade of the Davis Homestead. Below, the northwest side. The el at the right is where John Lawrence Davis, then a widower, was living in the 1980s when Emily H. Lynch of the Stonington Historical Society spent afternoons with him helping him sort his essays and reminiscences.

Sally Shaw, Mrs. John Lawrence Davis, in a fetching black straw hat, about 1920. She was born in Scotland in 1901 and emigrated with her family as a child. Until the 1926 auto trip to Vermont, John Lawrence Davis writes, none of them had visited outside of the Pawcatuck-Westerly area. Sally Shaw died in 1979.

John Lawrence Davis and one of his many horses, about 1920. He left school at 16 and by 1921, when he and Sally were married, he was running the farm.

CHAPTER 2

OLD FRIENDS, OLD TIMES

When I was about seventeen years old, I used to go hunting with John Schiller. We had each received guns of our own at the age of sixteen and were duck hunting at Osbrook Point in the bay. We would borrow Uncle Sam's skiff at Willow Tree Cove, row wherever we wanted to go to set decoys. We got there about daylight, set the decoys, and were hidden in the blind. It was a beautiful morning, still and calm. There were no ducks visible until we saw one lone sheldrake coming up the bay. He was out of gunshot range, but set his wings and headed for the cove back of the point. John said he would crawl over the top of the hill and see if he could sneak up on it and maybe get a shot. He got there pretty quick, I thought, but didn't pay too much attention. Just then I heard someone coming. It was Schiller. "Did you get anything?" I asked. He looked scared and funny. "Come with me," he said. I climbed out of the blind and up the bank following, him up the hill.

The grass was thick and heavy from all the summer growth and about knee-high. He stopped and pointed to the ground. "See that small hole in the grass?" he said. "Just get down on your stomach and look through it." I did. It looked like the path of some small animal. It was about twenty feet long. "What is it?" I asked. "Well, I'll tell you. I was crawling along on my stomach dragging my gun beside me with my right hand. I moved forward on my left side and then brought the gun forward. It went off just about four inches from under my chin. That hole in the grass came pretty nearly being a hole in me." We both became real sober then and vowed to be very, very careful in the future. A bush or stout briar had pulled the hammer back just enough to fire the shell.

Schiller told me about another time he was in a duck blind with two or three other fellows. They had their decoys out and some ducks came in, set their wings, but didn't light, just kept on going. The boys all cocked their guns. Two fired but the other didn't. In the excitement, he didn't let the gun hammer down. No ducks were hit and when the fellows settled down to wait for more, this chap's gun went off among them all. No one was hurt, fortunately, but it tore the top off of one fellow's rubber boot. The fellow whose boot was torn looked down to see what a close call he had had and promptly fainted. Schiller filled his hat full of water and threw it in the chap's face to bring him around. When he arrived home, his mother wanted to know how he had torn his boot and he told her he had caught it in a barbed-wire fence.

One of the big events of the winter, and one which we always looked forward to with great anticipation and pleasure, was filling the ice house. The ice was stored in layers with hay and sawdust to keep it through the summer, when it would be needed to fill the large iceboxes in the milk room. It was brought from the ice house by oxen, a whole cart load at a time. The boxes were filled to capacity and we always had plenty of ice if we had had a cold enough winter. If we didn't, then the ice had to be purchased from a dealer who brought it from Maine by freight-car load. He delivered it to us for $6 per ton. We used about one and one half tons per week.

After a cold spell of a week or so, Uncle would tell me to go down to the pond with an ax and ruler and cut a hole in the ice large enough to stick my hand into. I would roll up my sleeve, push my hand down through the hole and bring my fingers up against the bottom of the ice and hold them there. Then I would measure from the top of the ice down to my fingers and that would give me the thickness of the ice on the pond. He wanted at least six-inch ice. Seven- or eight-inch would be better. A horse had been sharpshod in readiness and the ice plow sharpened. Uncle would use a square and a long rope for the first mark. Then we would plow the ice almost through, plowed both ways in cakes, which, if I remember correctly, were three-foot squares. We couldn't plow too deeply or the horse would have fallen through. What was left to cut was done by a man using an ice saw. Long chutes were placed from the pond to the ice house and the cakes were drawn up the chutes by a grappling iron shaped like a double hook, attached to a rope which went through the ice house to a horse which pulled on the other side. Once the hooks slipped off the top of a cake as it got to the end of the chute, jumped in the air and hit Charles Babcock in the mouth and knocked out two of his front teeth. It cost $16 to get new teeth.

When the day came to actually fill, the entire neighborhood turned out. Having made all preparation beforehand, we hoped to fill in one day. Everybody came. It gave them a little extra money, which would come in handy and it afforded them an opportunity to visit with each other while they worked. For us boys, it meant staying out of school and having a high time with the men. Each of us had his own job to do and it was like an assembly line. Some sawed, some poled the floes of ice cakes to the chute where another split them in sizes to go up the chute. About three double cakes was a load. Another carried hooks from the house back to the water again, and so it went, all day long. By late afternoon, the house would be full, the chutes taken down and placed on rocks to keep from rotting. All this was done before the men went home. I have just looked in my farm diary and the last time the ice house was filled was February 6, 1917, with eight-inch ice.

One man who worked here at the farm I would like to write about was Samuel Tefft. He was a Civil War veteran and had been wounded seven times. He was always good to me and set a good example of how to be a man. I profited greatly by his teaching. He liked me and I liked him.

Around 1910 or 1911 he came to Uncle and asked if he could move a small cabin about 12 by 16 feet from Watch Hill over to Willow Tree Cove and live there. He would help Uncle on the farm, pay rent, or anything, for the use of the land for his cabin. He had a wife and family but didn't get along with them, so went on his own. His children were all grown and married, so he just lived on his pension from the service and enjoyed himself. He had enough to eat and plenty to drink when his check came in and he would stock up for a month at a time. He was no drunkard by any means but he would drink a bottle of gin or two the first of the month and then be cold sober the rest of the month. He was very proud of the Union Army and insisted on being called "Uncle Sam." So Uncle Sam he was to all of us. He was very proud of his skill and endurance in working and could keep up with any of us although he was over seventy years of age at that time.

He loved pets and kept from five to fifteen cats all the time. He fed them eels and fish, which he caught in the river, and when the cat population got too big for him to feed he had me go down with a gun and knock off seven or eight that were particularly wild. And they were wild! When a stranger approached the cabin, they seemed to climb all over each other's backs as they rushed out the door to hide in the brush or woods. Uncle Sam didn't work regularly, only when we had extra work to do such as haying, hoeing, cutting corn, carting manure, etc. Uncle never asked him anything for rent and paid him when he worked. But Uncle Sam was always bringing us clams, eels, and fish and would never accept any money.

I remember once Uncle Sam was filling his pipe. He cut off the tobacco from a plug, a piece about the size of a walnut. Then he rubbed it between his two hands until it was very fine. He then pushed it down firmly into the bowl of his pipe and put the stem into his mouth. He scratched a big Birdseye match on the seat of his pants, lit his pipe, waved the match in the air to put it out, threw it on the ground and put his foot on it. He then looked at me solemnly and said. "Johnny, don't you ever smoke." "All right, Uncle Sam, I won't." I said. And I never have. I have never been sorry about it either. Uncle Sam was a good man.

When I was big enough to drive a horse on a horse rake in the hayfield, sometimes I wouldn't rake just where or the way Uncle would have and he would correct me in a way that might be thought a bit severe. Uncle Sam would say to me, "Johnny, I guess the old man (as he would refer to my uncle) is more scared than hurt." I always felt better when he said that. On a farm you can't make too many mistakes; they are very costly. My uncle had very little patience with people who made mistakes. He used to tell me, in no uncertain terms, not to say "I thought," but to be sure you know.

I well remember one night, soon after I took on the farm business. I was washing the cows' hind quarters and tails to clean them of dried manure, etc. I was using soap and hot water and a lantern to see by. Now Uncle would never allow a lantern in the barn for some time or other it might fall or tip over and that would be bad. However, I set the lantern close by the stable door, firmly on the floor out of the way. Using all my pail of hot water, I had to go to the house for another.

Expecting to be gone only a few minutes, I thought it would be all right to leave the lantern where it was in the barn. I stepped out the stable door and then stopped. I thought to myself, I THINK it's all right but I am going to KNOW it is, so I set the lantern outdoors away from the barn. When I returned a few minutes later, I opened the barn door and was met head-on by one of the cows that in some unknown manner unstanchioned herself and was walking up and down the platform where the lantern had been. That was a time my Uncle's teachings surely paid off.

He used to have a lantern with a bull's-eye that would shine a light twenty feet or more. It hung on an iron rod stuck in the ground outside the stable door. This light shone down the row of cows and gave light for milking during the darkness of early morning. He used to milk at 3 a.m. when we sold milk at Watch Hill.

Uncle Sam used to have a vegetable garden at different places around the farm. One time it was in the Plum Bush by the large corn field. Part of the meadow was in hay and we were loading it on the oxen cart. I was driving the oxen and Uncle Sam was loading the cart. John Schiller was with us and he wandered into Uncle Sam's cucumber patch looking for one to eat. Uncle Sam saw him searching among the vines and called sternly, "Schiller, do you know what 'to Hell' means?" Schiller looked up surprised at the question and said he guessed he did. "All right then," said Uncle Sam, "you keep to Hell out of that garden."

Around 1919, I think it was, Uncle and I noticed a tall column of smoke rising back of Stony Pasture hill. I galloped down on horseback to see what it was. It was Uncle Sam's cabin. He had fought it as hard as he could by bringing pails of water from the river, but to no purpose, it was completely gone. The old man's face was all blistered and burned. I asked him how it had started and he said he had been sleeping and the first thing he knew his whiskers were on fire.

He notified his sons in Westerly and they took him back to live with his wife. He seemed perfectly content to do so. After I was married, I would get him to help me with hoeing. He was always a good man and lived to the age of ninety-two.

I have a nice picture of Uncle Sam standing in the doorway of his cabin. The picture was taken around 1916. He was always teaching me something. How to grind and whet a scythe. How to grind an ax. And how to splice a rope and tie a bowline knot — the greatest knot in the world, it never jams and can always be untied easily. Uncle couldn't splice a rope and before Uncle Sam came around, he used to take our sweep rope to a neighbor, Captain John Brewer, to be spliced when needed.

There used to be a man named Ellery Crumb who had a foxhound and who was a great hunter. He used to keep the foxes cleaned out around Lower Pawcatuck and Wequetequock for sure. His dog, that he trained himself from a puppy, would stay on a trail all day long. Ellery was very fond of woodchuck meat and would shoot one with his .22 rifle, dress it off, build a hot fire in Uncle Sam's cabin cookstove and cook the chuck. Woodchuck is nice meat, tastier than chicken. One particular day, Ellery had a very fine chuck. He skinned and cleaned it carefully and hung it up on the outside of the cabin, while he and Uncle Sam got the stove going. They visited together while waiting for the heat to come up, then Ellery went out to get the chuck. As he told the story later, he said, "I'll be gol-durned if the cats didn't eat up that woodchuck before we could get the fire going to cook it." Ellery never used profanity, but would come out with "gol-durned" when he was particularly exasperated. Uncle Sam agreed with him heartily, it was enough to make a minister swear. The next week, Uncle Sam sent out a call for help and Ellery and I went down there with our guns and cleaned out eight more cats. Then things settled down for a while, back to normal.

Skunk meat is good to eat also. It is dark and fat, but the fat dries out in roasting, leaving the meat quite dry. The oil is good for lame joints, coughs, colds, etc. A skunk has to arch its back to fire its protective musk. I catch them in a stone deadfall and they hardly ever fire. October, November, and December are the months skunks are best, as they are fat before hibernation.

When I was a boy, trapping during the fall and winter months was a good business. Skunks were as high as $3.50 and $4 for #1 grade and #4 grade went from 50 cents to 75 cents. Muskrats, 40 cents to 60 cents each and mink, $15 to $20 apiece. Some men worked all summer at different jobs, fishing, the golf course, boating, gardening and farming, but in the fall, they took down their guns and traps and went into the woods for the winter. One trapper told me he made $994 in one winter-catch. Of course, he covered a lot of territory, using his car for transportation. I have only trapped here on our property for the fun of it. Once I sent some skunk oil to Vermont for someone with a lame knee. Skunk oil can be purchased in a drugstore, but it has been treated in some way and loses its potency and is not as good as the pure, fresh oil.

A man named Ernest Lamb moved into our neighborhood from Ledyard around 1915 or 1916. He was a vegetable gardener in the summer and trapped all winter. He said when he was in Ledyard, he and another young man used to hitch up a horse to an old express wagon and start out about nine o'clock in the evening. Each had a good skunk dog they worked. When one got tired, they would put him in the wagon and send the other dog out. They walked the horse along back roads while the dog would be hunting the fields and woods each side of the road. When the dog barked, they would rush over and kill the skunk. They would do this until daylight.

In January one year, they had almost 1,000 skins. Ernest and I used to hunt deer and trap foxes together. He took a trapping magazine and sent for special traps and bait. He caught a lot of fox. When we had snow, Ernest would go out in the woods in the morning and from the tracks would locate deer. They would be bedded down in some swamp or thicket for the day. He would be careful not to disturb them and would return home. I would stop at his house on my way home from the milk route and we would make our plans to get one. One time, he was really excited, and said he had a buck located in a thicket at Osbrook and that he was a big one. Tracks as big as cows'.

We would need help on this hunt to be sure we got him so I called Henry Stewart to come over for the afternoon. The Stewart farm adjoined ours and we worked together hunting deer. Whit and I also helped them when needed. We all met here and then started for Osbrook. Arriving there, Lamb took charge of arranging our stands. He placed me way down by the bay and Whit and Henry on more open ground on top of a small hill but in different spots. If the buck came against that line one of us should get a shot at him. He then went into the thicket to drive him out. I took my stand behind a large oak tree that offered good concealment. I had my 25-20 rifle, with which I had made some very good shots and also some very bad ones. I estimated where the deer might come out and adjusted the sights on the rifle for that distance. Soon I heard a faint "whoop" that was the signal that Lamb had started him. A few minutes later I saw him coming, not fast but with big leaps. He was headed for the shoreline, which would take him out of our sights. Then he turned and started to run between Henry and me. I followed him along in my sights as best I could and fired. He stopped suddenly and hid behind some thick bushes.

I didn't know if I had hit him or not, but I could see a part of him through an opening in the brush about the size of a dust pan. I took quick, careful aim at that patch of hide and fired again. I could hear the pluck of the bullet as it struck. The spot disappeared. I put in another shell and waited. Nothing happened, so I walked along the path hurriedly toward the spot where I had fired. No deer! I circled wider and then I saw him, he was as dead as a doornail and the biggest deer I had ever seen. It being February, he had shed his horns, so I didn't get them for a trophy. I yelled to the others and they all came running. Ernest seemed amazed that I had shot the buck and shook my hand and looked at me in wonder. I asked him why it was so strange that I had shot the deer. "Why," he said, "you know why I put you way down there? Because I knew you are the poorest shot in the bunch and I didn't think he would come this way at all." Then they all laughed. I did too. I had the deer.

The buck was so big we couldn't get him into the car we had gone down there in, so we went back to the farm for the pick-up truck and it took all four of us to load him into it. I hung him on a tree and took his picture before I skinned and dressed him.

Incidentally, this was the day I accepted the appointment of district forest fire warden for the Town of Stonington. I held it for two years and then went back to being deputy warden. District warden required too much time. I was forest fire warden in Stonington for twenty-nine years and during that time I had many interesting experiences. I had crews from the high school, boys I trained as they came along in school and joined my crew. We had to pass state inspection and then were listed as a state crew. We were called out to fires as far away as Groton and Lantern Hill and sometimes a fire would burn for three or four days and nights.

In the '30s and '40s there were only three fire companies in the entire town, Stonington Borough, Mystic, and Pawcatuck. The rest of the town was taken care of by the state. There were five state wardens. Each district warden selected his own deputy who had to be approved by the state. They tried to get a crew organized in each town and I had charge of the Stonington crew. I took no fooling around from the boys. They worked hard and obeyed me instantly or they were fired from the crew. I had only one boy who didn't measure up. I had left him to guard a section of the fire line and he went home without reporting to me. Needless to say, he never came back.

The wardens were trained at state meetings that were held every March. Training instructions were given by state and deputy fire wardens, with lectures and blackboard drawings on what to do and how to do it. Crew men earned a little more than "pick up" men. Pick up men were the ones already at the fire when we arrived and would work with us to help put it out.

I first took the job of warden for protection of the farm. The first of May in 1930 or 1931, a fire started on the Highlands from a passing train. It swept down across the fields and woods to the Schoolhouse Four Corners where it was stopped by a road. The next day it started again and got to the Pawcatuck River on the east side and down to the West Woods where it burned two large henhouses owned by William Whewell.

We stopped it at the edge of our wood lot. There was a high wind blowing and I had a man, Jim Anderson (more about him later), on the roof of the barn with all the pails and cans we had, full of water. Pieces of burning shingles from the henhouse as large as your hand were blowing everywhere. Russell Stewart was bringing home a load of hay he had bought somewhere and when he saw the fire, he unhitched his team, leaving the hay safely up the road. He arrived home just in time to tear some shingles off the side of his barn where they had caught fire. Schiller's house also had a narrow escape that day. The state furnished fire-fighting equipment, so I took the job.

A year or so ago, I was sitting in a car uptown, waiting for Whit to finish an errand, when a car drew up ahead. A young man got out of the car and came hurrying over to me. He took something from his pocket and held it out to me. "See that," he said. "Yes, I see it. What is it?" I inquired. "That," he said, "is a state fire warden's badge. I have been promoted to a state job and now travel the whole State of Connecticut. I am chief of the North Stonington fire company and am doing just as you used to do. I have a high school crew that works like a clock. At first, they didn't think it would work when I suggested it, but we have been going for two years now, without a hitch. I wanted you to know about it as I owe it all to you."

"How come? I didn't give you the badge," I said.

"No," he replied, "but you trained me so I could get it and I want you to know I appreciate it."

"Gee, Senior," said I, "you were always a good boy when you worked for me on the farm, you were a good boy on the crew and you are still a good boy and I congratulate you on your success." I shook hands with him and he went back to his car and drove off. It made me feel good to have boys come back and thank me for things like that. Many have done so.

Around 1905 and 1906, we always used oil lamps for illumination and did so until electricity was installed in 1924. At that time, a man named John Donahue came around with a horse and wagon selling kerosene. He had a tank on the wagon with a faucet from which he drew the oil to fill our five-gallon cans. The stores didn't handle kerosene then and John did a good business going from house to house. He was Irish and had a nice brogue that I liked to hear, as it was so different from our diction. I remember one time he was late in coming around and we were out of kerosene. Father got out some candles his mother had made before oil was used and we used them for a week. I studied my lessons and went to bed by candlelight. I thought it was great fun. I would lie in my crib facing the candle that was left burning, half-close my eyes and the candle flame would appear to lengthen and grow taller. Then I would open my eyes and the flame would return to normal. The next thing I knew it would be morning. The oil Mr. Donahue peddled was called Lenox, so we called him the Lenox oil man. How I loved to hear that man talk.

While I am on the subject of kerosene, I would like to relate something that might be of interest. One winter day I was visiting a very old man who lived alone and who burned wood in an air-tight stove for warmth and cooking. I had bought a pig of him and after loading it we went into the house to get warm before I started for home. I was a young fellow at the time. The fire was low in his stove and he got a bottle of kerosene to bring it up quickly. "Davis," he said, "I am going to show you something you should know about using kerosene." The fire was low, not blazing, just smoldering. He opened the top of the stove and tossed in a few drops of oil. The fire began to give out a thick, gray smoke. "Now," he said, "never pour oil on gray smoke, as that is full of gas that will explode." He lit a match and standing back, threw it into the stove. There was a flash and the fire broke into flame. "See," he said, "that was the gas, and if I had poured in a large quantity of kerosene, it would have blown us both up. Now watch." He took the bottle and holding it over the fire poured some directly into the flame. It increased the fire until the flame almost touched the bottle, but there wasn't any gray smoke. "When you have gotten rid of the gas in the gray smoke, you can use the oil freely, but watch out for that gray smoldering smoke."

That was a valuable lesson to me and I have always followed that rule with the best results. But NEVER use gasoline on a fire. I threw some on a pile of burning brush from a coffee can one time, and as the gasoline touched the fire, a streak of flame came right back through the air into the coffee can, which I had emptied in one throw. It was a good thing I had emptied it, as the inside of the can burned up in my hand. Wow, I learned something then, for sure.

If I have a talent for remembering things taught me, I also remember many things my father said to me. One evening

I was sitting on the arm of his rocking chair studying "The Village Blacksmith" by Longfellow, which we had to learn to recite for school. We took it a bit at a time until we could recite the entire poem. When we came to the line, "And looks the whole world in the face, for he owes not any man," my father stopped me and said seriously, "Son, that is the way I want you to be. Owe not any man." I have owed men at times, but I have always paid them in full. It gives you a very satisfied feeling.

As I think back now, I remember a motto that hung on the wall of an insurance company office in Westerly. It said, "Live each day so you can look every man in the eyes and tell him to go to Hades." I am reminded of the man who asked his neighbor if his credit was good. The neighbor replied that he thought it must be good as everybody had it. Another time, on the arm of my father's chair, he said to me, "Son, all throughout your life, I want you to always remember to be a gentleman." "I never will be able to," I replied, "because I never will have enough money." "You don't have to have money. Remember, if you don't have a cent in your pocket and are dressed in rags and are without shoes on your feet, no one can stop you from being a gentleman." I have always remembered what he said and how he said it. I have always tried to live up to it and hope I have succeeded.

Mother was quite a churchgoer and my sister and I had to go to Sunday school. On special occasions such as Children's Day, Christmas, etc., we kids were called upon to make a recitation of some sort. I had a poem I recited once. I hated it, but I did it more or less satisfactorily I guess, and did not have to be prompted once. After more than sixty years, I still remember how it went. Father and mother drilled and drilled me until I had it to their satisfaction. It went like this:

> *It happened on a certain day*
> *A little fellow full of play*
> *Drew forth a sharp and shining pin*
> *Found a chair and pushed it in.*
> *He placed it with its point upright*

And thought it would be a funny sight
To see someone choose the chair
And start up hurt and screaming there.
Time passed on and Rex forgot
The danger of the cushion spot
Till tired out with play, he heard with glee
His mother's summons, "Come to tea."
He smiled to see the goodies sweet,
With eagerness, he took his seat
Then rose a loud and startling cry
And wild with pain, he bounded high.
Poor Rex, what hurt you in the chair?
Why, here's a pin, I do declare.
Rex hung his head no word he spoke
.But sore, repented his joke.
And now children dear, just one word more.
Let all unkind jokes be o'er,
For all unkind things we do
Are sure to get us into trouble too.

There had been no rehearsals at the church (the Baptist Church, which has been torn down), so I had no idea what was to come, other than my own. I waited with fear and trembled until my name was called, then stepped forward on the platform and spoke my piece. When I finished, everybody clapped politely and I felt both gratified and relieved. I was finished and could now enjoy the rest of the program. The next act almost took my breath away. A girl about ten or eleven years old (I was only six) came out from back of the curtain dressed as a fairy. She had wings that came out from her shoulders and she carried a wand on the end of which was a beautiful spangled star six inches across. Her dress was white with gold sprinkled throughout. The piano started to play and she began to sing. Now I had never seen a fairy, although I had heard about them, and I made up my mind that if they were all like her, then I was all for fairies. She was beautiful. I never knew who she was, where she came from or where she went, but I will never forget how surprised and excited I was when she burst out from behind that curtain. After the show was over, we had cake, cookies, and ice cream and then went home. The ordeal was over.

Ase Carpenter and his wife left here around 1906. The folks went away into town one afternoon and left Sade, Ase's wife, here cleaning the house. She not only cleaned the house, she also cleaned out a bottle of whiskey that she found in the bottom of the wardrobe where Father kept it hidden away for medicinal purposes. When the folks arrived home late that afternoon, Sade had reached a drunken, quarrelsome stage, so Father put her out of the house. She felt so ashamed about it that she wouldn't stay any longer. So Ase left with her.

He came back with another Negro who had just come up from the South and was looking for work. He had a wife and three children. Father and Uncle hired him and he stayed for fourteen years. His name was Thomas Burrell and he was a good, honest, reliable, hard-working man. We got lots of work done and raised good crops while he was here. One year we husked 682 bushel corn. He had a big garden, 2½ acres, raising beans and potatoes for himself for the winter. He also had a cow and some pigs.

He was a good man with the oxen. The oxen did all the heavy work at this time as we didn't have draft horses. We didn't use draft horses until 1926. They were faster than oxen and could be controlled easier. I could drive oxen all right, but the hired help couldn't, so I got rid of them and bought horses. I miss a good yoke of oxen though, they were all right. When I started with draft horses, I kept two teams. The first was a good young or middle-aged team that worked nearly every day and the other was an older pair that did the light work and were for beginners and kids to drive.

Tom had a son, Clyde. Clyde and I were great friends and had lots of fun hunting and working together. In October of 1916, Uncle and Aunt Bess (his wife) went to Springfield Fair and were gone for two nights. Clyde and I took care of the farm. We cribbed 134 bushel corn in one day. While Uncle was away that year, the big hotel called the Watch Hill Hotel burned to the ground. It was in the early evening and it was

On December 29, 1917, when fierce cold struck, Clyde Burrell, son of a worker on the farm and a friend of John Lawrence Davis, went duck-hunting on the frozen Pawcatuck River, got into a boat without oars and drifted helplessly. Davis, using the farm's oxen, eventually pulled the boat ashore. Westerly Sun for December 30, 1917

so bright you could see to read a newspaper by, here at the farm.

On the night of December 29, 1917, it turned suddenly very cold. The morning of December 30, the river was frozen over. The only open place was at the Narrows, and that was frozen for about one hundred feet from shore. Clyde went duck hunting that morning and killed two ducks at the Narrows. Unable to get them without a boat, he yoked up Dan's oxen, went to the dock, hitched on to a skiff and hauled it over the snow to the Narrows. The tide was out and the ice was on the shore from high water mark to the low water mark and beyond. Clyde unhitched the oxen from the skiff and pushed it out onto the ice. It began to slide down to the water's edge. He jumped and before the boat got away from him he was out on the river. Looking around, he discovered he had left the oars on the shore. Not daunted by the lack of oars, he pulled out one of the seats and paddled out and picked up the two dead ducks. By that time, the ice had formed quite thick on his paddle and when he got back to the edge of the ice he found it so thick there he couldn't break a path through it to the shore. The wind was blowing hard from the north and it was very cold and cloudy. It looked like snow, and it did snow all afternoon. With no shelter from the wind, out on that open river, Clyde began to freeze. A Mr. George Champlin, who lived on a farm near the Narrows on the Rhode Island side, saw him and his predicament. He telephoned to Dan (Davis) and told him about it. Dan said he couldn't do anything, to let him get out by himself.

Then Mr. Champlin called Uncle, who told me to get down there as quickly as I could and do something about it. I mentioned back a ways about hauling ice up the chute with a long rope. This rope hung in our shed on a peg all coiled up. I ran out to the shed and taking down the rope, I went to the river as fast as I could. Arriving at the river, I found the oxen patiently standing there waiting and Clyde was at the edge of the ice about one hundred feet from shore. I think if he had had the oars, he could have made it, but it was too far to throw them to him and his hands were so stiff, he couldn't have held them anyway. I shook out rope enough to reach the boat, carefully coiled it in my right hand, stepped to the very edge of the low tide mark and cast it as far as I could toward the boat. It went out to the boat, but missed it and Clyde couldn't reach it. I pulled it back to shore and then had to use the other end for my next cast as the rope end I had used was as stiff as a board where it had gotten wet from being in the water. I coiled it again and cast it out to the skiff.

By a stroke of good luck, it fell across the boat. Clyde's fingers were so stiff and numb he had to tie a knot as big as a bushel basket by using his wrists, pushing the rope through with his stiff hands but unable to pull the knot tight because he couldn't close his hands. I tied the middle of the rope to the ring in the oxen yoke, backing the oxen down as far as I could toward the water.

When Clyde was ready, I slowly took them ahead, the rope tightened, the boat came up onto the ice and then got stuck. I stopped the oxen and called to Clyde to get as far back in the stern as he could. I again tightened the rope slowly, the bow came up onto the ice and stayed there. It was easy after that. The oxen brought the boat right up onto shore.

Clyde slowly stepped out and took off for home. He was so stiff he could hardly walk. Tom went into the woods to chop that morning but returned home as it was too cold to chop wood. He and Clyde arrived home about the same time. Tom got a pail of snow and Clyde kept his hands in it until they thawed out. He saved his hands and fingers by doing this. I untied the rope from the ring, coiled up what I could and dragged the frozen part home. I unyoked the oxen thinking they would go back to the barn themselves. I couldn't drive them yoked as the bottom of their hooves were covered with ice and it made them slip going across the small patches of grass and small patches of ice on the marsh, over which they had to go to the upland. They were afraid of the ice and stayed there until Dan went down that afternoon in a snowstorm and succeeded in getting them to the barn.

When I got home, my cheeks were burning from the wind and cold. I put the rope back in the shed and then went into the house to get warm and tell Uncle the story. As I passed the thermometer hanging on the side of the house, I looked to see just how cold it really was. The thermometer registered twelve degrees below zero. Now that may not seem too cold, but it was cold enough for us.

Clyde was quite a boy. One time Tom was splitting wood at our woodpile by the crib. Tom's house was over in the lot west of the barn, quite a distance away. Suddenly a bee buzzed by his head. Then another bee passed by him. Tom thought it peculiar that bees were so active in the winter. He kept on working until there was a "zut" sound in the woodpile behind him. Tom stuck his ax in the chopping block, stood perfectly still and very alert. Soon there was another "zut" followed by the crack of a rifle. The sound came from his house. Tom followed the wall, keeping well out of sight all the way home. Clyde had a tin can on a big rock and was shooting at it with his .22 rifle. When he missed the can, the bullet came over between the two barns and ended in the woodpile. Tom took the rifle away from him and locked it up in the trunk. It was a long time before Clyde got the gun back. "Man," said Tom when telling me about it afterwards, "he could have killed me with that gun."

During the late '20s, I had a milk customer named Anderson. He had a son named James who used to help me around the farm and on my milk route. He was a good worker, was dependable, and never acted smart. He also never smoked. When he got out of school about 1930, he came to work for me by the month. He stayed with us for eight years and was like a member of the family. He never asked for a vacation in all that time.

We arose at 5 a.m. and planned to finish for the day about 6 p.m. In the summer we would work until 8 or 9 p.m. getting in the hay. I gave the boys Friday, Saturday, and Sunday off before Labor Day, making four days in succession to make up for the extra hours they had worked. Jim was big and strong and always right there when I wanted him. I had several other fellows during the time Jim was here, as I kept two boys or men by the month. We each had every third Sunday off, leaving two home to do the chores.

One fellow was very unreliable. He would work, all right, but you never knew when he would be back when he went uptown. After one of my Sunday afternoons off, I returned home to find the chores were coming along slowly. I stopped at the barn and found Jim doing the chores all alone. I inquired where the other fellow was and Jim was reluctant to tell me, but finally said he had gone home. Jim was quite upset about it but finally told me about what had happened. Jim had stopped by in his car to bring this fellow to work. He tooted his horn several times and waited and when the fellow didn't show up, he returned to the farm alone and started doing the chores. Finally the other chap showed up and started giving Jim a lot of "guff." Jim told him to shut his mouth or he would shut it for him. The fellow said "go ahead." So Jim did and knocked him flat.

The fellow got up and went home, he quit his job. Jim thought I would be angry about it, but I had had about enough of this fellow anyway. "Jim," I said, "I have only one fault to find with you about this." Jim waited tensely to see what the fault was. "The fault is, you didn't hit him hard enough. You should have knocked his head clean off." Jim relaxed and we finished doing up the chores together. The next morning, I went to the fellow's home to give him the wages due him. When he came to the door he had a piece of skin missing from under each ear. I asked, "How many times did he hit you?" The answer was, "Once."

I always gave the best one of my help $5 a month more than the others and held him responsible for the work when I was off. I retailed milk each day for forty-six years, so I had to be off the farm part of each day. Of course, Jim was boss the eight years he was here. He was always quiet and serious, but on occasion would clown around and make us laugh. I used to joke with him a lot. I would be serious at first to lead him on and then spring a joke. One time we were butchering lambs and Jim was right in the middle of it helping me skin. Now on the brisket, which is the chest between the forelegs, the skin is thick and tough and doesn't come away from the meat readily. I finished one lamb and went to help Jim with his. I watched him a minute and then began looking all around. "Have you seen that dog?" I asked Jim. He began to look around, too. "No," he said. I kept on looking. "How do you know there is a dog around?" asked Jim. "There must be a dog around," I said, pointing to where Jim had been skinning. "Look where he has been chewing on that sheep." Then how I did laugh. I could see by Jim's eyes that he was laughing inside too, but he only looked disgusted and told me to skin my own G— D— sheep.

During the 1930s, I had to make about a hundred quarts of milk a day. I sold seventy-five to eighty quarts on the milk route, made some cream, and supplied the West Broad Street School with twenty to thirty quarts per day in half-pint bottles.

In 1928, when I was going to Watch Hill (which was my last season there), I was milking twenty-three cows and getting 190 quarts of milk per day. It took lots of feed and I was compelled to hire some land as I didn't have enough of my own. I acquired all I could by cleaning out brush and plowing them after fencing them and then planted corn and millet. I selected about an acre in Stony Pasture and set Jim to plowing it in the fall. It was very stony and had never been plowed before.

Now Jim was always good and kind to animals. I can't recall seeing Jim ever striking or hitting a cow or horse while he was here. Sometimes he would verbally chastise them, but never physically. While Jim was plowing one morning, the phone rang and my wife answered it. Someone in Avondale, Rhode Island (across the river), wanted to know what the trouble was over at Stony Pasture Hill. "There's no trouble there that we know of," said my wife. "We have a fellow over there plowing, but everything is proceeding normally, as far as I know." "Well," said the caller, "I never heard such profanity in my life." When questioned about it, Jim said he was just plowing, there was no one there but himself and the two horses, and although it was a still and calm day, he didn't know his voice would carry that far. There were no more complaints and Jimmy plowed the entire piece.

Before Jim got a car of his own, his pals would take him around in theirs. One Sunday afternoon, the car was full and when they turned the corner on the River Road, they found they were going a little too fast to make the curve. The driver turned the wheel this way, that way, and the other way and this so confused the car that it apparently didn't know which side of the road it should be on, so settled the matter for itself by tipping completely over on its side. The boys opened the door on top and climbed out. None were hurt and the car wasn't even scratched. They all got on one side, lifted together and uprighted the car. Then they drove here to the farm, but not quite so fast.

I used to keep Guernsey cows as their milk was rich and made a good cream line on the milk bottles. Jim and I would go to the barn to do the milking in the morning and leave another fellow bottling it and carrying it down from the barn. I began to notice a much shorter cream line on many of the bottles and some of the customers began to notice it too. The boy who bottled the milk sometimes didn't want any breakfast. He just wasn't hungry. Jim and I suspected what was going on, so I changed them around and put the fellow in the barn. His appetite for breakfast improved immediately and so did the cream line on the bottles. He had been drinking the cream off the top of the cans, filling himself so full that he couldn't eat. There was no more trouble after that.

The Big Depression began in 1929. During the '30s, it was going in good shape. About 1933 or 1934, a Mr. George Chase came to me and wanted to know if I could use him on the farm. He was about sixty years old and had fallen off a ladder while picking apples and had landed on his back and broken it. This put him out of business for heavy or steady work. He had no home, so I built him a small cabin (12 by 14) down toward Osbrook Point, settled him in and he looked after the place. I moved the hens and hogs down there and he tended them in exchange for rent. It was a good little cabin with a cellar under it and a well for water. Jimmy was here and he and George became great friends. George would tell Jim about his travels. He had cooked aboard ships, been to China, etc. Jim figured up how long George had worked at different jobs and concluded that George must be at least 110 years old. However that may have been, George was a mighty nice fellow. I used to give him $2 a week for washing bottles and he received a food order from the town, for another $2. Four dollars a week may not seem like much, but when the State of Connecticut paid only 35 cents an hour for men to fight forest fires you can see what the economy of the country was then.

George also received a quart of milk a day and eggs, potatoes, and vegetables when he wanted them. He got his own firewood from the woods. During the Depression, I did much of my business by barter. Many of my milk customers were on W.P.A. and were only allowed to work three days a week. They would work for me the other three days for $1 in cash and a bushel of potatoes per day. Some worked their milk bill ahead for more than six months and had potatoes enough to last all winter. They were very pleased with this arrangement and so was I.

George was very faithful and took care of the poultry and hogs beautifully. In 1936, we raised 190 bushel potatoes, first and seconds, and 15 bushel of small ones for the pigs. We had 835 bushel of corn and George raised twenty-four turkeys, but the big thing was 200 Muscovy ducks. We only sold a dozen or so and ate all the rest. We would go down to George's and catch fifteen ducks and dress them off at one time, once a week. We would hang them up in the crib and Sally would cook five to seven at a time. Boy! did we eat. George had his share too. They didn't cost us anything as we raised the corn to feed them.

During the 1938 hurricane, George had his cabin full of people (ten or twelve) all night. They had floated across the bay on anything they could grab hold of and wandered up and found George's cabin. One lady had her wrist watch on and said she was just one hour in coming across the bay. George came up to the house here and got some tea, coffee and bread and went back through the high water and terrible wind to make ginger tea to warm them. None caught cold from the exposure.

George had been cook aboard ship and claimed he wasn't the best cook in the world and knew it, but he also knew there was no one who could cook any better. He used to make cake and cookies and bring them up to Jimmy who was loud in his praise and ate them greedily. One summer day, George brought a nice looking white vanilla cake to Jim. Jim cut himself a great big hunk and greedily started eating it. He nearly finished the piece and looking at George with appreciation said, "You really put on the dog this time, didn't you?" "What do you mean?" asked George. "Well," said Jim, "you put raisins in it this time. There are lots of them here." George pondered this for a minute and then said slowly, "No, I didn't put raisins in but the flies were pretty thick when I mixed the dough." Jim's face took on a funny look and he went outdoors. When he returned, the dog followed him to the door step and began to bark, apparently for more. George continued to make cake and cookies for Jim, but Jim looked them over very carefully before sampling them. George stayed with us until he was eligible for old age pension, which was 65. He moved uptown and we all missed him very much.

When Jim got a car of his own, he used to take his pals around and they would have great times. Jim also had a sideline that he called his "private business." He was very secretive and shy about it and I found out about it quite by accident. One Sunday morning when I passed by where Jim was milking, I casually glanced at him. Then I stopped short and looked at him closely. His face was a mass of cuts from shaving (cheeks, neck, side of face and chin). I never saw such a mess as he appeared to be. "Wow," I said, "you sure cut yourself last night didn't you? What kind of razor are you using? You won't be shaving again for a week until those cuts heal." "Look," replied Jim, "please don't interfere with my private business." It turned out to be lipstick. That was Jim's private business and I'm sure if he worked as hard at it as he did on the farm, he had no cause to worry. He would just have to succeed.

Jim's girl used to visit the farm occasionally for an outing to see the animals and, of course, to see Jim. One time she brought a package of which she was very careful. She carried it flat and had it in a large paper bag. Jim took it and carried it into his room. It was a beautiful cherry pie that she had made "all by herself," she proudly told him. Jim thanked her and started on the pie. He said it was darned good, but he had to eat it slowly as it was necessary to spit out the cherry stones at every mouthful. Jim had a big grin on his face and predicted she would learn.

When Jim left me, he went to work in the foundry in Stonington. When the foundry closed down he joined the Stonington police force and is now deputy chief. He is doing a wonderful job and is greatly liked by everyone.

To increase the farm income, other than milk I used to raise vegetables, such as squash, beets, carrots, lettuce, string beans, cucumbers, tomatoes, sweet corn, raspberries, and strawberries. Strawberries have to be set out a year before they can be picked, as the plants have to make the new bed to be picked. We lay a string across the field to be set to make the rows straight, then use a shovel to make the holes to set the plants in. The shovel is pushed into the soil the depth of the blade, then pushed back and forth to widen the hole. Then the hole is filled with water, the plant is put in with the roots straight down and the soil firmly pressed around it. The plant must be set so the crown is just out of the ground about two feet apart. We used to set four or five thousand each spring vacation, when we would get some school boys to help. (I am reminded that Ase Carpenter used to say about extra help that was hired from time to time, that they would come running, but would walk before they went away.) Now setting strawberry plants all day for three or four days is tiresome work, but it had to be done, so we all did it.

About the last day of setting, one boy named Thomas Sampson, who was a very good worker, finished his row, straightened up and, going to the stone wall, sat down on a stone beside the wall to rest a bit before continuing his work. He leaned back against the hard stones, let out a big sigh and said, "Boy, is this comfortable." We all laughed and remembering Stonewall Jackson in the Civil War days, we dubbed him "Stonewall Sampson of the strawberry patch." He still laughs about it and maintains those stones felt soft to his aching back. He never complained about the work being hard and he works just as hard today as a carpenter.

I would like to mention some of the things we used to do in the fall. October is, and always was, my favorite month. That is when we gather the harvest and get ready for the winter months. Corn, pumpkins, cabbage, turnips, apples, carrots, potatoes and onions all to be stored for the long, cold winter. Corn in the crib, pumpkins in the barn covered with hay and all the rest down cellar. The cider was made in October and how good that sweet cider used to taste and it still does. The "Minister's Barrel" was fixed with sugar and was always a treat for special guests. The air is cool and bracing in October, the woods are so pretty with their leaves of many colors, that everything seems to call, "Hurry, hurry, get ready for the cold, cloudy winds of November which precede the cold and snow of December."

We used to have husking bees in October. One group that came regularly every year was the Episcopal Church choir, about twenty-five or thirty of them. The minister was the Reverend G. Edgar Tobin. I remember when we were going to the barn from the house to start the husking bee, he asked where we were going. Pointing ahead of him, I said, "To the barn." "Well," he said, "it does look like a barn, but it smells like a stable." I guess that was his first introduction to what is known as a barn odor. We all thought it was a good joke and I have never forgotten it.

We had swept the barn floor clear of hayseed and placed a row of ears of corn to be husked from one end of the barn to the other through the center, about thirty or forty bushel. The huskers were on each side of the row and as they husked, pushed the husks behind them and put the corn in bushel baskets to be dumped into bags and set to one side out of the way. The ears were mostly yellow or white, but when a red one was found it entitled the owner to kiss the girl of his choice. The choir boys had previously loaded their pockets with red ears which were used over and over again. With some of the girls, they would not only kiss them on the strength of the ear, but would try to count kernels as well.

When the corn had all been husked, we would clear the floor again and have a Virginia Reel and a square dance. I would get a fiddler to play and some of them could "call off." On a big grain box cover, I had five or six gallons of sweet cider and drinking cups. They would be hot and sweaty from dancing and that cool cider tasted good. They would drink it all and then come down to the house for refreshments. Some brought sandwiches, others cakes, doughnuts, etc. We furnished the coffee and sweet cider and Sally, my wife, would make ten or twelve pumpkin pies, which were also served. They had all they could eat. I remember one pretty girl who, upon being offered a piece of pie by me, refused, saying she "had to watch her figure." I agreed with her and said I had been watching it all evening myself and I thought she was pretty smooth. How she did laugh.

When the refreshments were over, then the games would begin. They had a game called "Judge." A chair was placed on top of a large table, over which a tablecloth had been spread, one end reaching the floor in front. A stout rug was laid down, one end reaching under the table. A rugged fellow then hid under the table. Then two fellows would bring in a prisoner and stand him, or her, on the rug before the "judge," who would be sitting in the chair on the table. One fellow would hold the prisoner's arm to keep him on the rug and the other would stand behind him to catch him when he fell. The Judge would ask what the charge was and upon being told, he would give a jail sentence and order him to be pulled in. The fellow under the table would then pull the rug and the prisoner would fall backwards and be caught by the fellow standing there for that purpose. How the girls would scream when their feet went out from under them. Some of the fellows would be startled too.

Another game was "Fishing for the Dime." After the game of Judge was over, the chair and rug were removed but the tablecloth and fellow under the table stayed put. A large bowl was brought in about half full of tepid water, with a dime at the bottom. Then a chamber pot was brought in with about four inches of warm tea in it. This was kept under the table out of sight. The person who was to do the fishing and who had waited in another room, was told to come in and was shown the bowl and dime. Asked if he could pick the dime out of the bowl he readily agreed and did so. It was easy. Anybody could do it. All right then, if you are so smart, let's see you do it blindfolded.

He was then blindfolded, turned around a few times while the switch was being made, and led up to the table. If he had any difficulty in finding the pot because of the blindfold, he would be assisted by having his hand placed in the pot for him. He couldn't feel any dime. It wasn't there. It is there, we will take off the blindfold so you can see. When it was removed and he saw what he has his hand in, loud was his reaction. He would jerk his hand up out of the pot and jump back, then head for the sink room to wash his hands, accusing everybody of all the dirty tricks in the world. The crowd would just roar with laughter. Upon being told that it was only tea (some wouldn't believe it), he would calm down a bit, then grin and sit down and wait for the next victim. Each year the choir would have some new members to play it on and did they play it!

A few of the members, who come to mind after so many years, were Millie Higginbotham, Dave Laurie, Walter Krebs, Otto Findeisen, Ernest Young, Earl Saunders, Jack Opie, Mrs. Charles Larkin, the church organist and choir leader, Fannie

Brucker, Madeline Murray, Ida Findeisen, Donald Friend, Charles Larkin, Sr., Stanley Higginbotham, Ben Peabody, Eddie Fontanna, and George Anderson. There were many more, but the names fail me at this time.

And so life goes on at the farm. Sally and I live in the old wing and our son Whit, his wife, Hazel, and their two youngest children, Lawrence, aged twelve and Carolyn, aged five, live in the "new wing." They have two married children, Susan, the mother of two boys, and John Carter, the father of a girl, who have moved from the farm into homes of their own.

Larry (Lawrence) is in the 4-H club and has won numerous prizes with his animals, as well as his showmanship. He was picked by the judges to represent this area, at the Big Fair of the East, the Springfield Exposition. But upon learning of his birth date, he was too young by seventeen days to qualify, so couldn't go. We were all terribly disappointed, he most of all.

Larry is well versed in all phases of farming that I have been practicing for the past sixty years. I have taught him how to tie all kinds of knots needed around a farm, to milk by hand, break horses, do vegetable gardening (when to plant, how to plant, how to fertilize, etc.) and he has a garden of his own.

At the present time, we have two Morgan horses, fifty-four head of dairy cattle, twelve to fifteen sheep, two breed sows and one boar, one purebred Belgium stallion, mares, colts, thirty breeding geese, ducks, and chickens. Our farm was approved by Cornell University as a good place for young students to train for the veterinary profession.

I am hoping Larry will carry on in the footsteps of his forebears to keep the legend of the Davis Farm intact.

Miss Carrie Ryder and the pupils she taught at the Lower Pawcatuck School at Four Corners. John Lawrence Davis had started school a few years before, in 1905, at the age of seven, but there is no way of guessing which one is he in this picture, which he prized "very highly."

CHAPTER 3

SCHOOL DAYS

I started school when I was seven years of age. I walked to the Lower Pawcatuck School at the Four Corners, about a mile away. There was a family named Emmet living down by the river. Iasimina, Horace, and Katherine Emmet would come up to the house and go with us to the Schillers, where we would meet John and Mary and all go to school together. My first teacher was Miss Edith Burdick and she taught for one year.

When we returned to the one-room school house the following fall, a very different looking teacher was sitting behind the desk. She was large, heavy, and big boned. Her name was Miss Palmer. At nine o'clock she rang the bell and we all took our seats. She had drawn a map of the schoolroom with the rows of seats plainly marked and also each seat in the row. She told each of us to stand up and tell our names and where we lived. She marked this information on the map opposite our seats. In this way, she could call any of us by name just by looking at her map. She seemed nice enough and as she was strange to us, we also were strange to her.

Next, she asked all boys who had jackknives to raise their hands. She selected two, I being one of them and Harry Burdick the other, and asked us to come forward. She asked us if we knew of a place where maple had been cut recently. "You know those red sprouts that grow from the stumps?" We answered, "Yes, just down back of the school." "All right," she said, "you take this yardstick and cut me four of those pretty red sprouts.

One the size of a lead pencil, one the size of my little finger, one the size of my forefinger, and another the thickness of a broom handle, all three feet long. Think you can do that?" Then she gave us a warm smile. Eager to please her, we hurried to the swamp and selected the sticks she had asked for. "I wonder what she wants these for," asked Harry. I replied I didn't know but that we should pick out the prettiest ones anyway. Upon arriving back at that school, she next requested we cut a shallow circle around each stick about one inch from the end. When we finished doing that task, she tied a piece of string around each stick in the groove we had cut, then drove four nails in the wall about six inches apart and hung up the sticks. We returned to our seats and she addressed the whole class, with a very stern look and severe voice. She said, "Now I have a stick for the size of each child in this room and if you think I don't mean business, just you start something." Needless to say, we walked on tiptoe and were afraid to turn around.

One day at noon, when the teacher was out to the toilet and Harry and I were alone in the room, I said, "Well, Harry, we know what she wanted those sticks for, don't we?" "Yes," said he, "but you know something? She isn't going to club me with that broomhandle one." So saying, he grabbed the stick from the wall and with his penknife blade he cut a circle around the middle of it almost to the pith and hung it back up. We then went out to play with the other kids.

Some of the games we played in those days were:

Bull in the Ring. We formed a circle holding hands tightly so the bull in the middle couldn't escape. When the bull did escape, the other players would take after him, and the one catching him would then become the bull.

Horse. For this game we used a piece of clothesline about fifteen feet long, doubled it and put the middle back of the neck, then over the shoulders and back under the arms to form the reins. The driver then picks up the reins and is able to steer his horse by pulling either right or left. We used to race our horses around the schoolhouse to see who could get back to the door first and be the winner. I used to have a big girl for my "mare." Her name was Ruth Billings. Boy, could she run. Going around the corners, I would swing way out. It was all I could do to hang on. What fun we had.

Drop the Handkerchief. Boys and girls played this together. We would form a circle without holding hands. The one who is "it" runs rapidly around the outside of the circle and slyly drops the handkerchief behind someone. He keeps running and the one who has the handkerchief tries to catch him. The chase stops back where the handkerchief was dropped. Number two keeps running and drops it in back of number three. If number three fails to see the handkerchief in back of him and number two completes the circle, then number three is pushed into the circle with the title of "stinkfish." He stays there until someone takes pity on him and throws him the handkerchief. Then he comes out and runs around the circle again.

Duck on the Rocks is played by setting a stone on a rock and then knocking it off by throwing another stone at it. This was all right until the stones missed and hit some of the kids in the legs. Then we didn't play any more when the teacher was around.

The girls used to play hopscotch, skip rope, and house.

The boys wrestled a lot and played baseball. In the winter when there was snow, we would have some real good snowball battles. We would start out with equal numbers on each side. As one was hit, he would go over to the other side and so on until there would be no one left on one side. This used to take some time and a lot of snowballs. If the girls got in the way, we would turn on them with the snowballs and drive them back into the entryway. Sometimes, they wouldn't close the door fast enough and some of the balls would crash against the inner door. Then the teacher would come out and things would quiet down, but we always accused the girls of attacking us first. Then the teacher wouldn't know who to believe.

One day, about a month after school opened, one of the older boys committed some infraction of the rules laid down by Miss Palmer. It irked her to the point of giving him a beating. He being a big boy, she used the big stick. She grabbed the boy by the left wrist with her left hand and brought the stick down smartly across his shoulders and back. The stick promptly broke in half and went flying across the room. Miss Palmer was surprised, as was everyone else. She looked at the piece she held in her hand and saw where it had been cut. Then all "Hades" broke loose. Who had cut that stick? Nobody knew and there were two who positively did not know. Believe me, we were sure of it. After things cooled down a bit, she again sent Harry into the woods for another broomhandle-sized stick. When he returned, she accepted it and as he turned to go back to his seat, she gave him a wallop across his shoulders that brought tears to his eyes. Harry was a good brave boy and in World War I he volunteered to carry a message through a gas zone. He died from the gas, but he got the message through first. Miss Palmer only taught for one term and we all felt glad to see her go.

When the winter term began on January 1, we had a new teacher. We all had a great interest and curiosity to see what she would be like. In appearance, she was very young and very small. Probably didn't weigh over a hundred pounds. Her name was Miss Carrie Steadman and she came from North Stonington. She had a wonderful personality, which continued all her life. She later taught at the West Broad Street School in Pawcatuck until she retired as Mrs. Walter Reith.

When she rang the bell at nine o'clock, we all took our seats and waited. She had a pleasant voice and she got all our names and where we lived. Then she sent two boys for a pail of water down to Mr. Holland's house a short way from school. She asked us to help her in remembering our names and then she sent another boy for some coal from the coal bin. She asked why the four sticks were hanging in back of her desk and after we told her, she took them down, saying they would not be needed any more.

She taught through to summer vacation and there wasn't a kid in school who wouldn't have turned themselves inside out for her. As a reward for being good (not dropping pencils, closing pencil boxes quietly, not throwing spit balls, not whispering, walking quietly etc.) she gave out little slips of paper with "perfect" written on them. When you saved up ten, she gave you a penny. I have some of those "perfect" slips in my pencil box now, here at the house, that I have saved all these years.

The next fall we had another teacher, Miss Carrie Ryder, also from North Stonington. She was a very nice lady and we all liked her very much. The only time I ever saw her face as black as a thunder cloud was when she sent Albert Rogers and Ted Billings down to the Schiller farm for water. The school didn't have a good well, so our drinking water had to be brought in from nearby houses, usually the Schillers or Hollands. One carried the twelve-quart pail and the other the broom. When the pail was filled with water, the handle was raised and the broom slipped through. Each boy took an end of the broomhandle to tote it back. It made the load light and what water spilled didn't touch either boy.

From the schoolhouse window you could see halfway to Schillers. We were given a reasonable length of time to go down and back, but if we stayed too long questions would be asked and explanations would have to be given. Ted and Dutchy, as they were called, apparently stayed their time out. Miss Ryder went to the lookout window and seemed very intent on something she saw down the road. We all wondered what was going on. Finally, she turned back from the window and in about five minutes the boys came in with the water and set it on the shelf in the entry. We all drank from the same dipper. Ted and Dutchy came and took their seats. Several kids raised their hands for permission to get a drink. All were promptly denied. "I'm sure," said Miss Ryder, "that Edward and Albert, having walked so far in the heat, carrying that heavy pail of water, must be very thirsty and I want them to have the first drinks as their rewards." Both boys began to look scared and said they had a drink when they filled the pail, they didn't want any more, couldn't drink any more if they tried. Miss

Ryder was insistent and said, "Come, come boys, just taste it, anyway." Ted and Dutch turned white. They just couldn't move out of their seats. She waited a few minutes and let them squirm some more. Then she went to the entry, took the pail from the shelf and put it on the ground. Coming back, she sat at the desk and wrote a note, enclosed it in an envelope, sealed it and called two other boys. "Take this note to Mrs. Schiller," she told them. "Do not fill the pail until after Mrs. Schiller has read the note." They departed on their errand and soon we had another pail of water that we could all drink. The kids all questioned Ted and Dutchy, but they said they didn't know what was the matter. Later I found out. Ted had told me. It seems they had to urinate and it hit them just about the time when they could plainly be seen from the schoolhouse window. Miss Ryder must have seen the whole thing. They set the pail down, backed off about six feet and tried to hit the pail. Both made a bull's-eye. The water was a bit off color, but they brought it along to school anyway. I have spoken to Ted about this many times and we still have a good laugh, but he didn't want to take the first drink.

Miss Ryder had the sense and foresight to have a picture of herself and the school children taken in time for each child to have one on the last day of school before summer vacation. I prize this picture very highly. Miss Ryder taught the girls to be ladies and the boys to be gentlemen, or at least she tried. Throughout my life, I have remembered a poem she made us learn and put in our copybooks. I don't know as I have always lived by it but at least I have remembered it, so think I should get some credit for that. I set it down here for the benefit of others and advise them to give it serious consideration. It is:

> *Do all the good you can*
> *To all the people you can*
> *In all the ways you can*
> *As long as ever you can.*

Miss Ryder taught for two or three years and then another room was added to the school on the side facing a former addition which had previously increased the length of the original building. Grades 1, 2, 3, and 4 were in the side room with a teacher named Miss Edith Cook. She was very patient and nice with the little ones. She also was from North Stonington.

Grades 5, 6, 7, and 8 remained in the old part of the building. Miss Ryder was followed by Miss Carpenter, a nice lady from Beach Street in Westerly. These two teachers stayed until the fall of 1913 when the schools in the town of Stonington were consolidated and grades 6, 7, and 8 were transported to West Broad Street School in Pawcatuck. The small side room was abandoned and the five remaining grades were taught in the large room with a Miss Barry as teacher.

Miss Carpenter was a good teacher and did a lot for the school. The town refused to furnish new furniture, such as new desks, chairs, etc.; the old ones were completely worn out. Miss Carpenter got the kids interested and we all went out selling "Larkin Soap Orders" with the result that we got new desks, chairs, pictures for the walls, and a beautiful clock that was fastened to the wall for all to see at any time and a big, new dictionary on a stand. How I hated that dictionary. Every time we didn't know the meaning of a word, she would make us look it up in the dictionary. She would wait impatiently while we did this. If we gave up in disgust and said we couldn't find it, she would reply, "It isn't because it isn't there." We knew that, but it didn't seem to help much.

When I went to West Broad Street School, I was in the eighth grade and had a wonderful teacher, Miss Susan McMahon. She taught there several years and was greatly loved by every one. Upon graduation from grammar school, I went one year to Westerly High School. I attended Stonington High for several months and then stayed home on the farm.

The Thread Mill in Pawcatuck. Although life on the Davis Farm makes the nearby nineteenth-century spinning and weaving mills of New England seem distant, John Lawrence Davis indicates how close these river-powered industries really were in his chapter about Caroline Hazard. Mrs. Hazard, an African-American woman thrice widowed, picked vegetables on the farm as one of many ways to survive. Davis writes that she would always stop work at noon, when she heard the whistle blow at the Thread Mill on Mechanic Street, up the river. In some early directories, the address of the Davis Farm is given as Mechanic Street rather than River Road or Greenhaven Road, as at present. Beyond the mill, the Pawcatuck flows past the farm, into Little Narragansett Bay and the Atlantic. (Photo courtesy of the Westerly Library Archives)

CHAPTER 4
CAROLINE HAZARD

Back around 1904 or 1905 I remember an old Negro lady (and I mean lady) who used to pick vegetables for my father here at the farm. She was part Indian, was tall and thin, with straight hair which she wore in a bun at the back of her neck. Wisps of gray hair would protrude from under the brim of an old straw hat someone had given her and which she would tuck back in place whenever it needed it. She always went barefoot in the summer.

She had been married three times and had lost all her husbands. The first man was named Holmes, the second was Perry Hazard, and the third was Joe Bent. Left alone, she had a difficult time getting along. She lived in a two-room house which was built on a bluff on the Pawcatuck River. It was built into the bank and was stoned at the backside and both ends. The part facing the river was boarded up.

She worked at whatever she could do: washing, housework, picking vegetables or huckleberries, which she sold. She never asked for charity but people were always giving her things and helping her out. She had a lot of respect and everyone respected her for it. She never complained. She used to come to the house and ask Father if he had any vegetables she could pick. He usually did, so she would take baskets and go to the garden.

At twelve o'clock, the whistle at the Thread Mill would blow for noon. Her name was Caroline, and a few minutes later, she would come to the doorstep and sit down. There was a maple tree by the corner of the house which cast some shade over the doorstep and it would be cool there.

Mother would have dinner ready to put on the table and Father would bring a pail of fresh water from the spring well for dinner. Mother would say, "Cad, did you bring your dinner today?" Caroline would say, "I am not very hungry today so I didn't bother." Guessing that the old lady probably didn't have anything to bring, Mother would say, "Don't you think you might eat a little something if I fix it for you?" "Well, Miss Ida," Caroline would reply, "I'll try if you want to give it to me."

Mother would fill a plate with boiled potatoes, johnnycakes, string or pole beans boiled with pork, cucumbers sliced in vinegar and seasoned with salt and pepper, and a slice of bread with butter. "Won't you come in the kitchen and sit up to the dresser in a chair instead of on that hard doorstep?"

"No, Miss Ida, it's hot in the kitchen and cool out here. I would rather sit out here," Caroline would say.

Mother would pass her plate out the door and then we would sit down to our dinner. (Of all the times Caroline came over I never remember of her coming in the house.) When we finished eating, Mother would go to the kitchen for dessert. That was usually Jell-O. Jell-O was a powder with different flavors, strawberry, cherry, etc. You would dissolve it in a dish of hot water and let it cool. We liked it served with cream or without the cream.

Passing the screen door, Mother would look to see how Caroline was doing with her dinner. She would be all through and Mother would say, "Well, Caroline, you did eat a good dinner after all, didn't you?" Caroline would then say, "Well, Miss Ida, I didn't know I was so hungry. It tasted so good. Thank you so much. I feel a lot better." Mother would ask her if she could eat a bowl of Jell-O. "I don't know, Miss Ida," Caroline would say, "but I'll try." Mother would give her a dish and she would eat it all.

After she finished, Caroline would reach into the pocket of her dress and take out her corncob pipe and a can of Prince Albert smoking tobacco. She would proceed to fill her pipe and light it. When it got going to her satisfaction, she would ask Father if he would like her to sing him a song. "Sure I would," Father would say. "What are you going to sing?" "Gillhouley's Party" was the answer. "All right, let her go," said Father. Then Cad would begin:

"Oh, Gillhouley gave a party to some friends awhile ago, there were knives and forks and spoons and girls and fellows and men and their wives, and I never saw such a devil of a time as there was around that night."

Another song Caroline used to sing was "Where Did You Get That Hat?" Caroline's voice sounded like a crow with a very bad cold but it pleased the lady and Father was loud in his praise.

"You know, Cad," said Father, "I made up a poem about you the other day." "Did you, Mister Al?" Caroline would reply. "I sure did," said Father. "What did it say, Mister Al?"

It went like this, said Father.

> *Caroline Holmes, Perry Hazard, Bent.*
> *She opened the door and out she went.*
> *She ran so fast that when she slipped*
> *She skinned her HEEL.*

This pleased the old lady so much that she requested Father to tell it to her about every time she came over. She never tired of hearing it. She was so complimented that someone thought enough of her to write a poem about her.

Father went on the milk route to Watch Hill every day. Sometimes he didn't get back eleven o'clock or so. Then he made out the books which told what each customer had had that day. Sometimes he wouldn't finish until noon and Cad would be sitting on the doorstep. Father would change from his milk route clothes to those he wore around the house. He would come from the bedroom looking for his overalls which had been washed and were hanging over the stove to dry. He would prance by the screen door where Caroline was sitting in her usual place on the steps. "Now Cad, don't you peek. Don't you peek," Father would say. The old lady would say, "No, I won't peek, Mister Al. Honest, I won't." And she would laugh and giggle like a school girl. How Father and Mother would laugh at her embarrassment.

Caroline would go down to Charlestown, Rhode Island, to visit with her relatives. Sometimes she would stay two weeks or more. One winter she made a two-week stay in February. She took the train from Kingston back to Westerly and arrived in the evening. Why she took such a long time to return nobody knows. But she did. It was right in the middle of a northeast blizzard, only instead of snow it was rain, a freezing rain. It just poured, with gale winds to drive it. She got someone to telephone to my cousin, Fred Davis, asking him to come to Westerly to get her and bring her home. Fred said he was not going out in such weather, for her to go to a livery stable on Coggswell Street where the owner kept a room to use when it was cold and where he was waiting for the owners of teams to come for them. It had a bunk, stove, lights, and fuel for the stove, and was warm and cozy. He would get her the next morning.

The next morning, he went to the livery stable but she wasn't there. The livery man had not seen her and didn't know anything about it. Fred came back and stopped at Caroline's house. She was there, in bed, and sick from walking three miles home in the gale winds and cold rain. The roads were all mud, and it's a wonder she got home at all.

Poor Caroline passed away soon after that, but those who knew her had fond memories to remember her by. Caroline's gravestone in the cemetery at the bend of River Road reads: "Caroline Bent, wife of Perry Hazard, d. April 18, 1908, aged 88 years." (Perry died in 1900, also 88 years old).

Now I would like to add some history regarding the room at the livery stable. It was used frequently by people who came to town Saturday nights and wished to stay over until Sunday morning, when they could go home. Two such boys came one evening from North Stonington. North Stonington is five miles from Westerly and walking that distance over frozen, rutty roads in the dark is no picnic. The boys decided to stay all night and go home in the morning when they could see the road better. They went to the livery stable and asked Mr. Brown if they could stay in his office for the night. He readily agreed, so they stayed.

The next morning Mr. Brown came to the stable and rolled back the big door, went in and fed the horses their hay and grain. Then he opened the door to the office to see if his guests were still there. They were there, all right, but both were dead. They had been stabbed to death and robbed of what little money they hadn't spent the night before. Needless to say, this caused a great deal of excitement, but the mystery was never solved nor the murderer brought to justice.

Sarah Maria Davis (1856-1944), John Lawrence Davis's aunt, and sister of Alphonso and John Jeremiah. She taught at the Lower Pawcatuck school and once strangled a rat with her bare hands, according to her nephew.

CHAPTER 5

AUNT SARAH
(Sarah Maria Davis)

My mother and father passed away when I was nine years old. Uncle John became the guardian of my sister, Marcia, and me. Uncle's wife (Aunt Bess) and Uncle's sister (Aunt Sarah) helped. Both ladies had a great influence upon my life. Aunt Sarah lost her mother (my grandmother) the same time I lost mine and she then cooked and took care of us two children. She kept our clothes clean and well patched, cooked good wholesome farm food, and attended to our wants in any way. She used to tell us about when she was a little girl and went to the Lower Pawcatuck School, the games they played and the fun they had.

In May, they hung May baskets to each other. This would be a small basket filled with candy, cookies, cake, fruit, etc., decorated with colored paper. This would be hung on the door in the evening. They would knock, then run away and hide. The girls or boys whom the May basket was for would come out and find them. When all were assembled, they would come in and a social time would be enjoyed. Games such as Spin the Pan, Drop the Pillow, Post Office, and Chewing the String would be played. In Chewing the String, a piece about two feet long would be used. A girl would put one end in her mouth, a boy would put the other end in his. They would eat up the string until their lips met. What fun.

When the cows were driven home from pasture in the summer, some would be milked out in the barnyard as the small barn wouldn't hold them all at one time. Auntie used to get a pail and stool and milk one old cow which was very gentle. The cow didn't have to be tied and would stand perfectly still to be milked. Auntie would milk the cow out all clean (get all the strippings) and was very proud of the accomplishment. She learned from her mother about picking wild greens such as milkweed, dandelion, and Narrow Dock. These are all good when cooked with a piece of salt pork. The Narrow Dock is eaten with vinegar on it and tastes like spinach. The milkweed is eaten with butter and cream and the dandelion with vinegar.

Puffballs were gathered in the summer or fall and kept in the house in a paper bag. They were used to stop the bleeding of cuts, etc. A puffball was the only thing my mother ever used on me when I cut myself with a knife or knocked off a piece of skin. It always stopped the bleeding and healed nicely.

Aunt Sarah was always humorous and greatly enjoyed a joke. She was an old maid and she used to stress the fact that it was from choice and not from necessity as she had had several offers of marriage from nice gentlemen. But because her mother's mind had been somewhat affected when passing through the Change of Life, Auntie elected to forgo marriage and devote herself to the care of her mother. Auntie used to dress up as an old maid with curls and an old bonnet and recite at church gatherings and D.A.R. meetings about an old maid who suddenly realized it was leap year. The piece was very humorous and Auntie used to have lots of fun reciting it.

During the time of their fashion, she wore hoop skirts. These hoops, with a few pieces of fragile cloth still clinging to them, are in our attic now.

When Auntie drank from a cup she would always grasp it by the handle with her thumb and forefinger. Then she would raise her little finger out one side as far as she could. This was the dainty way a lady should drink from a teacup.

When I was about five or six years old, Auntie hung me a May basket one evening. Father and Mother made me go to the door as it was getting dark and I was afraid of the dark.

Finally we all opened the door together and there was the May basket. Among other things in it was a nice napkin ring. Inside was a paper on which Auntie had written this verse:

Put your napkin in the ring,
Morning, noon and e'en
And when you grow a mustache
Be sure to wipe it clean.

Up to the time I was sixteen years old, I was given 25 cents per week for working around the farm. Of course, I would have had to work anyway but the 25 cents made it easier. I was twelve years old when I got the chicken fever, that is, I wanted to have some chickens of my own. I wanted Barred Plymouth Rocks. They are a pretty bird.

One day, I saw an ad in the Poultry Item, a magazine devoted to poultry. I still remember the ad. It said, "16 Barred Rock eggs, $1. Ringlet strain. Bred for heavy egg production and show points, 6 firsts and 2 seconds at Honesdale. Cockerels for sale. Clarence Fortman, Tyler Hill, Pa."

I immediately saved up a month's wages and sent for the eggs. They came each wrapped in excelsior and packed in a basket. I set them under a hen and she hatched out eight chicks. Being something special, we put the hen and chicks in the front yard near the house. They were in a small house with a crate attached. When they were big enough, we pulled the crate away from the house just enough to let the chicks out but to still confine the hen.

One day, Auntie was washing dishes in the sink by the kitchen window. She heard a very loud plaintive peeping coming from the chicken coop. She went out to see what was causing the trouble. She saw a good-sized rat, which had one of the chickens by one wing and was trying to drag the chick into its hole in the wall.

Auntie cried "Shoo" and flapped her apron but the rat wouldn't let go.

Now, what do you think she did then? She did just this. She reached down, grabbed that rat with her bare hands and choked it to death! She didn't get a bite either. When I came home from school she showed me the rat. And the chicken, aside from having a bloody wing, recovered.

One day I got a new milk customer. His name was Lamphere and he had just retired from being captain of the Coast Guard on Block Island. He was a bluff, hearty man, good natured and generous to a fault. However, when he gave an order you jumped to obey. Cap had a little Boston bulldog which was always snorting and whuffing like he had a cold. He would wag his stump of a tail and go sideways and snort. Cap thought a lot of him however and said he was the d_____ dog he ever saw. "You know, Mr. Davis," Cap would say, "when I let him out of the house every morning he goes over to that tree and makes so much water you could be sure he couldn't make another drop for at least a month. He will lower his leg, walk slowly around to the other side of the tree, lift his leg again, and piddle a pint! I never saw anything like it."

Cap and I used to talk together quite a bit and one day he asked me if I was any relation of a Miss Sarah Davis who used to teach school. "Yes, she is my aunt," I told him. Cap's face broke out into a big smile and he said, "Well! You know I used to go to school with her and she was a wonderful teacher and a nice lady. I always hated school but I enjoyed it while she was the teacher. You ask her if she remembers me." I did when I got home and Auntie said she did remember him, that he was a good boy and never gave her any trouble. I told Cap and he was very pleased about it.

When Auntie was seventy-three years old, the flock of sheep, headed by a large ram, came from the back pasture and were headed toward the highway. Auntie saw them and went out to drive them back. She shooed them with her apron, then turned back to the house. Suddenly, the ram attacked her, knocking her down and breaking her hip in such a way that it couldn't be fixed. She went on crutches the rest of her life and my sister Marcia took care of her, night and day, for fourteen years.

Auntie was a good woman.

CHAPTER 6

AUNT BESS
(Elizabeth Hamilton Davis)

Elizabeth Hamilton Davis, my Uncle John's wife, came from Stonington, Connecticut. She was always good to me and treated me like a son. She was very clearheaded and practical, as was also my Uncle John. Uncle used to say, "Some fool would write a book. People would read it, believe what it said, and then they would become fools also." In this way they taught me to analyze things I heard and to think for myself, not to believe everything somebody glibly told me.

Sometimes, people would come to the house, shake hands effusively, ask if they could come in and the see the old house, large fireplace (second largest fireplace in New England), compliment us on everything in general, and then, just before leaving, ask if they could buy a piece of land of us so they could build a nice house down by the river. The answer of course was "No." After they had gone Aunt Bess would look at Uncle and say, "I wondered what they wanted. If they hadn't wanted something they never would have come here." He would laugh and agree with her.

I have had the same experience many times throughout my life, and it is always very interesting the way they try to butter me up so as to gain their point. Aunt Bess (while appreciating an honest compliment) looked upon flattery as being highly deceitful and would have none of it. Neither would Uncle.

Elizabeth Hamilton Davis of Stonington was John Lawrence Davis's Aunt Bess, wife of Uncle John. She got up at 4 a.m. to prepare food for a hungry family. Davis writes that she made most of the important decisions for the household, and directed him always to uphold the family honor. (Photograph by Brown Brothers)

We had a man by the month who ran the Watch Hill route. He got $35 a month plus room and board. His name was George Lee and he was a fine fellow, working for us four years.

Aunt Bess used to get me up when she got up at four o'clock in the morning. She would get breakfast for George by five o'clock, while I had to chase the horse to the barn from the North Pasture, where he had been turned out all night to feed. I had to harness him to the express wagon and have him at the door by five o'clock to carry the load of milk and vegetables down to the boat to go across the river to Watch Hill.

This was from 1911 to 1914. Sometimes it would be raining when I went for the horse and I would get soaking wet. The mosquitos would be thick in clouds. The horse seemed to know of my discomfort and would add to it by running all the way around the six-acre lot three or four times before going out the gate to the barn. Of course, I had to keep chasing him until I got him.

Sometimes I would go with George and then I would really have to hurry. I would eat breakfast with him. We had fried potatoes and beans, bread, milk or coffee, also brown bread. Aunt Bess could really fry potatoes and how good those beans used to taste. They were Yellow Eye beans cooked with salt pork and molasses. We never tired of them.

The teachings of Aunt Bess and her sayings had a very profound influence upon my life. When I was small she would tell me I was a Yankee. Not understanding, I resented the name and would make a fuss about it. Then she would look at me and tell me that some day I would be proud to be called a Yankee. She was right. She used to say to me:

Don't count your chickens before they are hatched.
There is many a skip between the cup and the lip.
Don't think you are the only pebble on the beach or the only tin can in the dump.
Always do your best, and when you do, be sure it is your best.
A poor workman always blames his tools.

Just before you did, you didn't.
It is an ill wind that blows nobody good.
A fool and his money are soon parted.
When you get to thinking you are pretty smart, remember this: You are only half as smart as you think you are.
Never sign a note for anybody. (This one saved me $2,000 one time. A fellow wanted to borrow $2,000 from a bank and asked me to sign for him. I refused. He went bankrupt.)
Never borrow money.
Never mortgage anything.
Make your head save your heels.
Remember, hard work never killed anybody.
Be honest with yourself, and you will be honest with other people.
Don't put all your eggs in one basket.
Don't cut off your nose to spite your face.
There are none so blind as those who will not see.
Remember, birds of a feather flock together.

All these sayings I have remembered and applied to my business as I could. They are all sound and have done me a great deal of good. She was a very wise person.

I was always small-boned and frail (I weighed three pounds when I was born). At school, beng so small, I was good to pick on by the larger boys. But I held my own as best I could. One fellow my age and size was especially troublesome. He could hit me at will but I couldn't seem to hit him. My chum and I couldn't figure it out until one day we discovered that he and his brothers had a set of boxing gloves which they practiced with all the time. That was it. They were trained and I wasn't.

That evening after supper I went in Uncle John's part of the house. Aunt Bess was washing dishes. I told Uncle I wanted something very much. He asked me what it was and put away the newspaper he was reading. I said I wanted a set of boxing gloves. He shook his head and said, "No." I asked why and he replied he thought I would get to fighting. I said I would not get to fighting and if I acquired any skill at all it would only be in self-defense. Never would I bully anyone.

Most major decisions were left for Aunt Bess. So in this case she asked me who had boxing gloves. I told her.

"Well," she said, and nodded her head up and down, "I think it would be all right for him to have them." Uncle looked surprised and said he would see. That Saturday Uncle called me in and said he was going to town for something and would I like to go with him. Would I? I guess so. Never was a horse hitched up so fast.

On arriving in town, he said he wanted to go to Willard's Hardware Store. Did I want to go, too? I did. We went in and he asked me to tell the clerk (a Mr. Burdick) what I wanted. It was a set of boxing gloves and they were $5. Uncle paid for them and we started home. On the way I stopped at the Schillers' house and told John I had them. He came down right away, by the time I had the horse unharnessed.

This was our big secret. We told nobody. We put them on in the kitchen and then held a council as to what to do. Neither of us wanted to rough it up as that would teach us nothing but rough stuff. We wanted to become skillful without getting hurt. We each placed a cap lightly on our heads and tried to knock it off. First we went at it in slow motion. We would slowly swing at the cap and then raise our arm to ward off the blow. That was it. We were both delighted. He and I boxed for years and never did we strike a blow in anger but we learned a great deal about boxing.

Nights, after supper, George Lee would get his corncob pipe, sit with his knees drawn up and his back against the house, and watch and criticize us as we boxed. He told us about footwork and never cross our feet or take our eyes off our opponent's eyes since you could read what he was going to do before he did it. Instead of swinging, we developed a straight punch which was more difficult to block. We would leave openings purposely to trick each other.

One night after John went home, George knocked the ashes out of his pipe and said to me, "You and Schiller get along pretty well together, don't you?" I told him we did.

In later years, while in the Navy on a minesweeper, John was forced to box a fellow his size one day when they were laid up in port. He knocked the fellow out in the first part of the first round.

I have only used my knowledge five times to defend myself, but during all five times, as the fellow said when he went to the toilet, everything came out all right. It gives you a feeling of confidence to have this knowledge, and I saw to it that my son, my grandsons, and godson all have boxing gloves.

If Aunt Bess hadn't said "Yes" I would not have had them.

When I was about fourteen years old I was at that age known as awkward. My feet were always getting tangled up when girls were around so Aunt Bess decided to do something about it. She sent me to dancing school. She also sent my sister. We went to Miss Penfield at the Wequetequock Casino for the summer. It was for beginners and believe me I was some beginner. When I began they all got out of the way. They would either be bumped into or stepped on, it didn't make much difference. I was dancing. I was learning to trip the light fantastic. When I wasn't tripping, my feet would slide out from under me and I would go down anyway. Mostly anyway. Sometimes, I would hang on to the girl and we would both go down. This got to be so embarrassing I would let go of the girl, throw both arms high over my head and go down alone.

But I kept on and finally got to the point where I could do it quite well, that is, fall gracefully. That was my own opinion; what others thought made no difference. I was having a good time. Dancing, I finally learned it well. I have Aunt Bess to thank for it.

In 1918 a fellow named Bill Rovelto visited here at the farm for three days. He had run away from home when he was fourteen years old, joined a circus and stayed with it for two years.

He taught me how to spin a rope, jump off and on a running horse, and to stand on my head on a horse. He was a nice fellow, didn't smoke or drink, was mild-mannered and quiet.

Before he left we put on the boxing gloves. I couldn't hit him but he could me. He was bantamweight champion of New England and got his title in the Boston Garden. He then showed me a lot about boxing, how to roll with a punch, how to draw your opponent up close to you and also how to keep him away. He asked me if I had ever been to dancing school. I told him I had and asked him why. He said my footwork was better than he had expected to find it. He also showed me how to shadow box and told me what it was for.

He also told me as long as I lived, not to even think of going into the ring, either for glory or for money. All you ever get is a terrific beating, and as for the glory, those who yell for you when you are winning will boo you if you are losing. He was a nice sensible fellow. I was pleased that he said my footwork was good. That was partly due to my dancing lessons.

I was jumped by a fellow who worked for me a few years later. He was out to clean me up. I remembered Bill's shadow boxing and he got cleaned up instead. After we were through he said he had a terrible headache and wanted two aspirin instead of one. We gave them to him. He was a very good boy after that. He worked for me a long time and we got along fine.

One day Aunt Bess said to me, "You know, there are two things you want to pay particular attention to throughout your life. One is your conscience, the other is your honor and the honor of your family. Remember that. You have a little voice inside of you that tells you when you've done wrong. It's there and you can't get away from it. When you do something that isn't right, your conscience will tell you. You will despise yourself. You will lose your self-respect and if you don't respect yourself, others won't respect you either."

As you go through life, you will realize how important this is. "Let your conscience be your guide" is no idle saying. And when you make a promise, be sure to keep it.

So, I owe Aunt Bess a great deal.

Lunch in the Green Mountains of Vermont, 1926. Sally Davis is on the left, over two-year-old Whit, who is digging in the lunchbox. John Lawrence Davis is having a sandwich and Sally's mother, Isabelle Shaw, is at the right. Photo was taken by Sally's father, David Shaw.

CHAPTER 7

VERMONT TRIP--1926

This picture was taken in October 1926, somewhere in Vermont's Green Mountains. My wife is at the left. Our two-year-old son is looking for something to eat in the lunch box. I am having a sandwich. The lady at the right is my wife's mother, Mrs. Shaw. Mr. Shaw took the picture. None of us had ever traveled beyond the Stonington and Westerly area when we decided to take a trip off into New England.

The car cost $350 with no self-starter. It ran on a magneto and we cranked it to start. Gas was 15 cents per gallon and a tourist's room was $2 per night. The car had side curtains which we put up when the weather was bad. We had a hot breakfast and supper but carried our lunch with coffee in a thermos jug. We made the coffee each morning where we stopped for the night.

We took $50 with us, planning to go north on $25 and come home on the other $25. This we did. We went as far as Napierville, Canada, on the first $25 then turned around at noontime and headed for home.

Coming home, we stopped the first night in Vergennes, Vermont. Mr. Shaw and I needed haircuts so we went to a barber shop that evening. The barber was a nice chap and we told him where we were from and where we had been. Mr. Shaw was proud of his Scottish ancestry. I said I was from Welsh stock way back but was born in the United States and my family had been here since 1772. We inquired as to his family history and he said we could call him what we liked but some of the people around there thought he must be a cross between a son of a bitch and a jackass. However, there was a twinkle in his eyes when he said it.

That was a wonderful trip, six days on $50. The road on Route 7 from Williamstown, Massachusetts, to Rutland, Vermont, was all dirt in those days. They were laying cement in one place we came to. They worked up one side of the road for about a mile, leaving the other side open for traffic. We lined up with twelve or fifteen other cars to wait for the southbound line to come through. The last car in line brought a red flag to the guard who was holding us up. Then we went through. The last car in our line took the flag to the other guard who let the southbound line through again. I remember we carried the flag going north. The dirt road was rounded a bit to let the water off from a rain or melting snow. A farmer told us that every five miles other farmers were hired to drag the road, each having five miles of road to care for. That kept the road smooth.

We always had to be ready for flat tires. Those Model T Fords didn't have demountable rims. The rim was a part of the wheel. To remove the tire we wedged it off with tire irons which were twelve inches long, one inch wide, and flat. After the tire was off, we patched the tube by roughing around the puncture with the top of the can which held the patches. Then we applied the jelly from a tube, removed the cloth from the patch and applied the patch to the tube. When dry, we put the tire back on the rim, blew it up, removed the jack, and we were on our way. Those cars had a thirty-inch-by-three-inch tire in the front and a thirty-inch-by-three-and-one-half-inch tire in the rear. Two sizes on the same car. I don't know why but that is the way it was.

CHAPTER 8

THANKSGIVING ON THE FARM

Back in the 1930s, along about the middle of August, the subject of Thanksgiving came up in the family — where it would be held and couldn't the whole family get together in one group in one place. I didn't get too concerned until it came out that it would be nice to have it on the farm. What a proper place for Thanksgiving — down on the farm, just the right atmosphere. Wonderful!

Now, I was the only one who had a farm. I rightly concluded that I was to be host to about eighteen to dinner that day. Now I raised and had ducks, geese, and chickens but some thought it more appropriate to have the traditional turkey that day, not ducks, geese, or chickens. So turkey it had to be and turkey which I had to buy.

In every family there are relatives and also irrelatives. The relatives are those whose opinions agree with your own and the irrelatives are those with whom you do not agree and so do not count. Now both kinds were to be there and I knew that if I didn't have enough turkey so that, after eating their pie, they could reach over to the meat platter and spear a small piece with their pie fork on which they could chew, uncertain whether they could swallow or not, being so full, then I would be censured for not having enough. And if there was not enough of both light and dark meat left over so that it could be divided up and taken home for the next day I would be doubly censured. This I had to guard against by all means.

John Lawrence Davis's Aunt Bess, Elizabeth Hamilton Davis, is photographed basting a goose in a portable oven set in the kitchen fireplace. This is one of a series shot for an article on Thanksgiving at the homestead by Brown Brothers for a magazine article, about 1906. Brown Brothers retrieved the original photographs for this new edition of the book.

Now, in buying a turkey there were two major requisites. It had to be big and it had to be cheap. Turkey at that time was the most expensive of any bird. Ducks, geese, and chickens were much cheaper. These I had but in this instance it had to be turkey. I did not have much money to spend so I didn't know where I could get a turkey. I pondered over it for several days and nights and then I had an idea. I would go to my good friend Nelson Wheeler who raised turkeys and see if he could help me. Nelson kept turkeys and hatched their eggs. The hatched poults were raised and sold for Thanksgiving and Christmas. I drove up to Nelson's and explained my problem.

Nelson said he had a really big tom turkey that was two years old but was fat and would cook all right. He was too big to sell to the trade so he would let me have him for 25 cents a pound alive. A real bargain! Was I pleased, I guess so. We went out to the turkey pen with some corn and Nelson dropped some on the ground and called, "Turk, Turk." The biggest gobbler I ever saw came over and began to eat the corn. Nelson handed me the corn scoop and reached down, grasped the bird by each leg and lifted him up. We carried him to the shed and weighed him: thirty-seven pounds, $9.25. Now I could feed them for sure. We tied his legs securely together and put him in a bag with his head out of a hole which we cut in the bottom for that purpose. I paid and thanked Nelson, wished him a Happy Thanksgiving and drove off for home.

Arriving at my cow barn, where I was going to keep the turkey until the next day before I killed him, I carried him in on the big feed floor, untied the bag and pulled him out. He just lay there and when I freed his legs he still didn't want to get up. I knew his legs had been tied tightly and that the circulation had probably stopped. I picked him up and held him between my legs with his feet touching the floor. Soon he was able to stand with me supporting him. I walked him ahead a few steps then let him go alone. He staggered ahead a bit then walked faster and faster, then ran and flew right through the barn window, outdoors, taking the window panes and all the sash with him. Cleaned the frame right out clean, not a bit of glass left. I went over and looked out just in time to see him light on the ground about one hundred yards away. I hurried out of the barn and down where he was. It was close to the shed where I keep the feed for the one hundred or more hens we had. I got some corn in a pail, threw some around on the ground and called "Turk, Turk" like Nelson did. No Turk. What I had now was a highly suspicious bird and then some. He eyed me like I was his most hated enemy. I scattered more corn around but the hens had all come around by this time and they ate it up as fast as I could throw it out. My gobbler didn't seem hungry at all, just picked up a kernel once in a while and kept his eye on me.

We played this game for fifteen minutes or more. Then his attitude changed. He seemed about to fly off. I had visions of losing my turkey altogether and then I remembered how my father and uncle used to treat birds they couldn't catch, mostly turkeys and guinea hens. I went to the house, got a double-barreled 10-gauge shotgun, slipped in two shells of No. 2 shot, put four or five more shells in my pocket for good luck and went back to the feed shed. My bird was still there but he was edgy and nervous, ready to fly off. The hens were all there too, looking for more corn, although they had had enough and were pretty well filled up. The turkey kept the flock between himself and me. I couldn't shoot with the hens walking around as I might kill some of them.

I got a whole twelve-quart pail of corn and threw it out all at once. The hens put their heads down to eat, leaving the gobbler standing up. I grabbed the gun, squat down and aimed for his head. Then I fired right over the tops of those hens. The loud sound of the gun so close to them scared the whole flock to the point of frenzy. They flew frantically in every direction. I guess half of them came straight for me. They bit me so hard I went over backwards as I was already in a squatting position. Their wings beat me on the head and body and their feet clawed my face, all dirt and mud. When I picked myself up there wasn't a hen anywhere in sight but my turkey lay on the ground right where I wanted him.

I ran over and bled him. He was shot in the head only, so there would be no pellets in his body. One of the drawbacks of shooting game such as rabbits, squirrels, and pheasants etc., is when you are chewing the meat and enjoying the taste, suddenly you bite down on a lead pellet and nearly break a tooth. For that reason I prefer to trap my game by using a deadfall.

I put the gun back on its rack in the house and returned to my turkey. Two or three hens had returned to the corn they left so suddenly but that was all. My face was all scratched where they had clawed me but I felt very pleased as I picked up my turkey and started for the barn where I would hang him up and pick him. I looked at the hole in the side of the barn where the window had been and wondered how much a new one would cost. Enough, no doubt.

Just then, that gobbler seemed to come alive. Of all the thrashing and pounding of wings there ever was, this was it. I let go of his legs, jumped back out of way and let him go and go he did. He thumped and banged for a good two minutes and then he stopped. I picked him up and carried him into the barn where I hung him on a couple of hooks over the stable gutter. These hooks were used to hold up calves or lambs while being skinned.

I began to pull feathers and was coming along nicely when the string which held him to the hooks broke and he fell down into the unclean gutter. I retrieved him from the mess. I then got a piece of small rope and again hung him up. This time he stayed. I finished picking and took him to the chopping block at the woodpile. There I chopped off his head and brought him down to the house and showed him all clean to Sally.

She took one look and then said she never could get such a big bird into her sized roasting pan. What to do now. I had a big bird like I wanted but no pan to cook it in. We thought of all the neighbors who might have one that we could borrow but gave them up as not having the proper size. The turkey all clean weighed thirty-two pounds. Then we thought of another fellow who was a caterer. He not only had a big pan but he volunteered to cook the bird for us. He did and made a nice job of it. The turkey was as tender and moist as could be. Everybody had enough and then some.

When I went for the turkey on Thanksgiving Day at noon and opened the roasting pan I saw that even if he did have a big roasting pan, he had to tie the turkey up tight to get him into it at all. Each leg had two half hitches around them which were tied to the stub of the neck. These were drawn up, bringing the whole thing closer together. Around his body was another stout string holding the wings close in. I thanked my caterer friend and brought the bird home in triumph.

None of the family had ever seen so large a turkey and all were in loud praise of it. We had oversized slices of turkey meat with stuffing, mashed potatoes, mashed turnips, boiled onions, cranberry sauce, pickled pear and mashed butternut squash. Dessert was apple, pumpkin, and mince pie.

It was a really wonderful Thanksgiving.

The homestead family posed around the table for the magazine story, a rare photo of the pre-1908 family. Starting at the near end of the table, the participants are Alphonso Whitman Davis (head bowed), John Lawrence Davis's father; on his left, John Lawrence's grandmother Phebe Mulford Davis; on her left, John Lawrence's uncle, John Jeremiah Davis; at the far end, Elizabeth Hamilton Davis, John Lawrence's Aunt Bess; the child in full view is John Lawrence's sister, Marcia Louise; and John Lawrence himself, probably eight years old, can barely be glimpsed behind his father. Note wall telephone at left and case of Indian artifacts at right. (Photograph by Brown Brothers)

*Garner's Bridge over a creek in the Continental Marsh, a field
of salt hay on the farm. Family tradition holds that this bridge
was built by an Indian known only as Garner, who worked at
the farm in the late 1700s or early 1800s. He built it using
three large flat stones for the top. Since then, John Lawrence
Davis writes, many "heavy loads of hay, wood, etc. have been
carted over it." (Photograph by Fred E. Burdick)*

CHAPTER 9

INDIANS

It has long been known that a tribe of Indians lived along the Pawcatuck River on the west bank. Anything definite about them however was not known, only things in a general way. There was, and is, a dancing ground located at Osbrook Point and supposedly there was a burial ground also. These two plots of ground can be seen plainly today. The dancing ground is entirely free of stone and is quite smooth. The burying ground is on a point of land directly by the river and is a succession of humps and well-defined hollows. The hollows were supposed to be sunken graves. There is a four-sided stone that protrudes about eighteen inches from the ground. This marked the grave of a chief.

Oyster shells, in various quantities, have been found all along the river along the shore and also in the fields and meadows. These spots of shell were accounted for in different ways. Some said they were oyster beds when the ice pack passed over the country and when the contour and surface of the country changed, these oyster beds were left high and dry on the land where they are now found. Others claim that they were early camps of Indians. No one seemed to give them much thought and they were taken more or less for granted.

In 1651, Thomas Stanton, who was called the "Indian Interpreter," built a house or trading post on the bank of the Pawcatuck River about one quarter mile northwest of the Pawcatuck Rock. The site of this post is marked by a boulder, cut with a face and lettered as follows: "Site of the house of Thomas Stanton an Indian Interpreter, 1651." Now Thomas Stanton must have been very friendly with the Indians and he would have located near them to trade. Hence, there must have been quite a number of Indians nearby.

This writer was always interested in Indians, as were his father and uncle before him. Numerous stone arrow points, axes, spearheads, pestles, and knives were found in the fields and gardens. These were sure signs that the land was hunted over by Indians but, nothing else ever having been found other than stone implements, it was believed by us that nothing else ever would be.

Certainly, no one ever thought of digging into the oyster beds in search of anything further. If the Indians lived here, they must have had teepees or cabins; some house or shelter to keep them from the cold and storms. They had, of course, rotted away long ago. Who could locate them and how?

The western Indians lived in wigwams made from the hides of buffalo, stretched over long poles set in a circle on the ground and coming to a peak at the top. A fire was built in the center and smoke went out through a hole left open at the top. Everyone knew this and, as an Indian was an Indian, of course they lived that way around here. The Indians were nomads and the skin teepee or wigwam could be moved at will and easily erected again.

In a vague way it was known that the axes were bound to a stick or club and used for hunting or warfare. The poor Indian was always pitied for his seemingly poor and ineffective weapons. The bow and arrow was all right in its way, but what a way. When you stop and think that he lived in the Stone Age period, with nothing but stone, the bones of animals that he killed and the hides and stones to work with and from which he made his weapons, clothes, things for pleasure and shelter, it's a wonder that he lived at all. The different tribes were always at war with one another and the Indian was always considered a fierce fighter but in what way was this war carried on? Did they have a war and then make peace or were they fighting all the time? What caused the ill feeling between the tribes? How did the old Indian cut his wood with only a sharp piece of stone hung on a handle? How did he fell a large tree for a dugout canoe and how did he hollow it out after he had felled it? These questions come to mind but how could they ever be answered?

The Indian was gone, his teepee was gone, nothing apparently remained but his stone implements. What stories these things could tell if they could talk. The great secret will always be theirs but an inkling of the truth has come to us through the influence and interest of Norris L. Bull of Hartford, Connecticut. He is making an archeological map of the state of Connecticut as it pertains to Indians and has a collection of Indian relics from the entire state in Hartford. If he had not wanted some relics from the Pawcatuck River valley what is known the tribe here, evidently a branch of the Pequot tribe, would probably never have been known.

William Beebe of Niantic, Connecticut, Mr. Bull's field supervisor, pitched his tent on the banks of Willow Tree Cove near Osbrook about the twelfth of August in 1931 and dug Indian relics for nearly ten weeks. He then moved to what must have been their main winter camp located about a quarter mile up the road from the Davis wharf. It was between two ledges where they were sheltered from the winds and had easy access to a fresh water brook that came out of the woods and ran into the river. From this campsite he excavated twenty-two perfect bone awls in one week.

In the following pages I shall tell of what was actually seen and will give my ideas as to how they lived, etc. Of course, these ideas are founded on what I have learned from Mr. Beebe and Mr. Bull, besides my own observation. Both of them agree that it would take two or three years to dig all of the Osbrook Indian camp thoroughly. I am carrying on the work as fast as I can and keeping in touch with them. It was agreed when they came here to dig that I was to have half of what was found on my land. I wish to thank them both for the fair way in which I was treated.

I shall never forget how I first met William Beebe. We had just finished unloading a load of hay in the afternoon and I had just come out of the barn. A stranger came toward me with a trowel in his hand. He was accompanied by a boy about ten or eleven years old. He asked me if I knew where there was a pile of oyster shells along the river or a spot where they were showing in the soil. I asked him what he wanted with oyster shells. He replied that they were an indication of an Indian camp and could I direct him to some.

Little thinking what would come of it and because he aroused my curiosity, I immediately led him to a shell heap on the bank of Willow Tree Cove. Here the shell showed in much profusion. He kept looking around the country with much interest and seemed pleased when I told him about a nearby spring. When he began to dig with the trowel among the oyster shells I thought he was a nut and when he found what he called a small piece of turtle shell, about the size of my thumbnail, I considered I knew it.

Continuing to dig, he brought to light more of it and it began to look like turtle shell as I have seen the cross section on the back of turtles. Bill, as I shall hereafter call him, then went close to the river where there was more shell and dug out a piece of bone. This he claimed to be a deer bone. I looked and wondered if someone had buried sheep there sometime. I voiced my thoughts but he only laughed and asked me if he could camp there and dig. Little thinking I should see him again, I told him he could and he went away.

About ten days later he came again, dug a little and said he was going to move his family down and live in a tent. I never took this very seriously until about the twelfth of August when he showed up with both family and tent. He said he was doing the work for Mr. Norris Bull of Hartford, Connecticut, and offered to pay me for the privilege of digging. I told him I only wanted half of what was found and he was welcome to excavate as much as he liked.

I went down to the camp as often as my work permitted and he invited me to dig and showed me what to dig for. One of the things found quite frequently was quahaug shells. These pieces of shell were quite hard and the Indians used them for scraping their arrow shafts, hides, etc. The pieces which they used show a rolled edge, caused by use. Some of them were used for scraping bone awls or fine points on something, for they had been cut into on the edge and used for just a certain width. Among other scrapers which we found were some made of stone, bone, and one deer tooth. The bone scrapers also showed a rolled edge.

It seems the oyster shell heaps were the rubbish heaps of the Indians. While they lost some perfect things among them, the broken pieces far outnumbered the whole ones. It is the lime in the oyster shells that has preserved the bone material for so long. The Indians obtained the quahaug clams from a bed around Hall's Island, which is at the mouth of the cove. Often the pieces of bone or pottery or shells, etc., fit together and we then glued them.

Bill was new to this place, of course, and he figured out the size of the Indian camp. They camped all the way from Osbrook Point to Pawcatuck Rock. Osbrook was their summer camp, evidently, although he found signs that they stayed there all winter as well. Their main winter camp was about one quarter mile from Davis wharf along the river between two ledges with a hill in the back on the north. It was open next to the brook on the south but sheltered even there somewhat. The brook came from the swamp and flowed to the river. We judged this to be their winter camp because of the amount of deer bone found there. Two complete skulls of deer with legs, ribs, and toe bones were found. They evidently had had a big feast.

The Indians camped beside the springs, brooks, and water holes all along the river. We know this because the oyster shells prove it.

All over Osbrook there have always been hollows in the ground ranging from a slight depression to fifteen or eighteen inches deep with a diameter from three to six or seven feet. They were similar to the graves on the burying grounds. Those away from the burying grounds have always been a mystery. Bill figured these hollows to be the site of Indian huts. The Indians dug a round hole in the ground the size they wanted their huts to be, which was not very large. Over this they probably made a low teepee, just about high enough to stand up in. Into this, they went in cold or stormy weather.

The dugout acted as a cellar. It seemed to enable the Indians to maintain an even temperature through all kinds of weather without the aid of fire. This must have been a very important item to the Indians because they had nothing to cut wood with in large quantities or haul it home except on their backs. I personally think this is one reason they moved around so much; they carried the fire to the wood instead of the wood to the fire. What dead wood they could find, they put on their fires and, as one end of the stick burned up, they pushed the rest of it on. In bad weather, they would go from their fire in the woods to their huts by the river, crawl into them and stay until the weather cleared. (This is what I think.)

In digging at Osbrook we usually found a top layer of soil, then a stratum of shell which varied from three to four inches to a regular pocket three feet deep. In these pockets was generally found the most stuff because the Indians built a fire here to roast their oysters, clams, and fish. In one of these pockets, Bill found a quahaug clam shell among the fish scales. The quahaug had been used and cracked, which caused the Indians to discard it with the fish scales. Bill brought it to me with the scales clinging to the shell. I glued the scales together and have both the scraper and the scales in my relic case now.

Another thing that is very interesting, and which we found quite a bit of, is pottery. This pottery was made of clay and shows that they were very skilled workers. We found several caches, big walls of clay up to the size of a four-quart measure, buried in the ground to keep it moist and fresh. Some of it had already been mixed with finely pounded oyster shell, ready for use. The oyster shell was used to make lime in the clay. Nearly all of the pieces of pottery found plainly show the fine oyster shell if you look at their broken edges.

Just how they shaped these pots is not positively known. One idea advanced was this: They formed a ball of reeds and grass the shape they wished the pot to be and then plastered the clay around it. The grass was then set on fire and burned out. Nearly all of the pottery found here shows the marks of reeds or heavy grass on the inside and sometimes on the outside as well. The inside of the pottery is black and the burned part seems to extend nearly half way through the thickness of the wall of the pot.

Another way they were supposed to make them was to roll the clay like putty into a round thick string or rope and then coil it around and around letting each fall on top of the other until they had the pot finished. They then baked it. The first method I think is the correct way.

Their pots were of different sizes and shapes and some were colored. I have pieces of a pot highly colored with red. I found an arrow point, in black soil, covered with this red substance. They had used it for a pottery marker. These pots were covered with different designs and ornamentation. Especially near the rims the Indians worked the prettiest part. I have now twenty different designs on pieces which we have found to date in my relic case besides the several beautiful pieces Mr. Bull took to Hartford with him for his collection.

Mr. Bull says they got the idea of one design from the Iroquois Indians in New York State as they frequently made their pots with scalloped edges. If so. this shows how much the tribes traveled around.

The nearest to a whole pot that I have is eleven pieces that fitted together. They comprise one fifth of the entire pot but show what the pot looked like. It was shaped very gracefully. Some of this clay pottery crumbles when it is dug up while other parts of it remain hard. They also made pots from soapstone. I have a piece of one such pot about five inches wide. On the under side is a grip or handle cut in the stone while at one end of the piece is a hole drilled through the stone. The Indians probably broke it sometime and drilled a hole each side of the break and tied it together with a piece of sinew. I have also a piece of clay pottery drilled the same way. The hole in the stone pot was drilled half way through from one side. then turned over and drilled to meet the first half. These drills were made of hard stone shaped like a slender arrow point and affixed to a handle or shaft. This shaft was then twisted once into a bow string and revolved back and forth rapidly, one man pressing down on the shaft and the other working the bow.

This same principle was used in making fire. Instead of a stone point a wooden one was used on the shaft. The friction caused by the rapid motion of the shaft in a piece of dry wood placed under the shaft caused some inflammable substance (like a mouse nest) to smoke and finally to burst into flames. The mouse nest was placed around the whirling shaft point. I have seen a man start a fire in this way nearly as quickly as I could scratch a match, so do not pity the poor Indian when he wanted to build a fire. He would do it while you would be thinking about it.

They did not hang these pots over the fire to boil water nor did they build a fire around them. They heated stones and put them into the pots of water. These stones made the water boil and they could then make their soup. The Indians evidently liked the marrow in the deer bone, for nearly all we find have been broken in small pieces.

It is interesting to note the different kinds of bones we find among these oyster shells, which have preserved them for us so nicely. We can see that this culture must be from 250 to nearly a thousand years old by the kinds of animal bones we dig up and the condition of the stone implements found. Bill found a broken celt (which is a pear-shaped ax with the wide end for the edge) which is rotten. I have spoken of the top layer of soil and then the shell strata. Below the first shell stratum, Bill found more soil of course but upon thrusting his shovel deeper he came to another stratum of shell. This clearly showed two occupations, years apart from one another. This celt was found in the soil below the second shell stratum and

Bill estimated it to be 800 to a thousand years old. It once was polished but now it almost crumbles.

When the Pilgrims landed at Plymouth in 1620 this land was inhabited only by Indians and wild animals. These bones take us back to that time and before. Who has heard of wild moose and bear in Connecticut? Yet we dug up three pieces of moose vertebrae and a piece of moose antlers in the year 1931 at Osbrook Point. The moose antlers are partly flat and it is the flat part that we dug up. We have deer antler and bones in abundance and also lots of deer teeth. We found very large teeth, both tusks and grinders or chewing teeth, which are so massive they must have come from a bear. Beaver were then here, for we have split pieces of beaver tusks and also what we believe to be a porcupine jaw. There are several other jaws yet to be identified. Bird bones as large as those of hens were found and also small bird bones and even their bills.

These Indians must have been good fishermen, for we found a piece of swordfish vertebrae. Swordfish are a good-sized fish and yet we must consider the fact that there were Indians on Block Island, who certainly must have had good, strong, seaworthy canoes. We find sturgeon shell also and numerous bones of smaller fish, including blackfish jaws. For shellfish, they had oysters, long clams, quahaug clams, mussels, and scallops. We have not found any crab or lobster shells to date.

The Indians had their fires in holes in the ground. This may have been to conserve the heat or to keep the wind from them. They also could roast their meat over them more handily as the heat would have had to come straight up, and it also made them a sort of oven. They dumped their oyster shells in these holes too and had their fires among them. This is evidenced by the charcoal found in these fire pits. The shells probably kept the dirt and mud from the coals. The charcoal is in pieces from the size of a lead pencil rubber to a piece as large as your thumb. These fire pits are mostly close to or very near large rocks. The Indians used these rocks for seats and could therefore sit around near their fires and tend to the cooking. They would sit on the rocks and eat their oysters and scrape their arrow shafts or make arrow points.

All around these rocks and extending out three or four feet from them the oyster shells would be sometimes two feet deep. Beyond them would be undisturbed soil. Around one rock sometimes would be found as many as fifteen to twenty scrapers. About six inches from one large flat rock we found a bone spear. It was about eight or nine inches long. Just above where it was dug up on the side of the rock was a small ridge. It had evidently been laid on this ridge and had rolled out and been lost.

Close by, near another boulder, were found four arrow points and a sharp-pointed knife. They were made of flint and had fallen down the side of the stone. Still another thing we found, beside a very large flat rock, was a lead bullet. It was all flattened out and down about six or seven inches in the shells. It had evidently hit the side of the rock and popped down beside it. This rock is about ten feet long, four feet wide, flat and about twelve inches high. It would have not afforded very good protection for a fighting Indian; it was too low. It may have only been a spent ball, but whether it was or not, it came from the direction of the river and, as each side of the river was hostile to the other, you can draw your own conclusion.

I have a handful of stone chips found beside one rock where the Indians sat and made arrow points. We found these chips all over the place but these were found together. The Indians made their arrow points of stone, bone, and horn. The arrows made of stone were chipped or flaked around to get their general shape first. Then they were flaked down to a point. The flaking was done with a bone or stone or antler.

Some of the celts and axes were polished as smooth as a piece of glass. Mr. Bull said that in some places he has dug he had found as many as two bushels of stone chips around a rock. This would indicate that they had special arrow markers.

I have three unfinished arrows found at Osbrook in my case and they plainly show just how they were made. I have also found several arrow-making tools which are just pieces of bone and antler. To make an antler arrow they used the antler tips, cut them off and sharpened the point. They then drilled a hole in the back of the arrow and stuck the shaft into this hole. We found another arrow with a hole partly drilled into the back of it for the shaft. In boring the hole, the Indians had split the arrow and then thrown it away. The pieces were only inches apart and they were all found and we glued them together. Sometimes they used the deer toe bones in the same way. The bone arrows were also ground to a point and then drilled for the shaft. Bill found a deer hind leg bone with the point of a stone arrow imbedded in it. It looked as though the deer had been wounded and had gotten away. Later, it had been killed. The bone had grown around the stone. Mr. Bull took this for his collection in Hartford.

I have often wondered just how the Indians hung their axes on a stick. The axes are quite large and have a groove around them where the handle goes. Some think they split a stick and slipped in the ax and then bound it with hide. However, this, as I have tried, doesn't make a very satisfactory job. It is weak. Another way is to place the ax on the handle as a grub hoe is placed, that is, with the edge crosswise. A thong can be passed around the axe with ends back on the handle and then wrapped with other thongs around the handle and repeated two or three times. If the ax was small, this would be quite strong.

However, the most generally used way, and I think with but few exceptions, was to take two green sticks, either hickory or white oak, cut them in the winter and use them right away. Consider how thick the ax is to be mounted, then tie a piece of sinew on the end of both sticks, fastening them securely but leaving them a little apart. Place the ax in between the sticks together and they will hold the ax as in a vice. Then bind the handles with hide. With a cross binding of hide around both ax and stick, it makes a very strong job. Mr. Bull says he has one in its original handle and it was mounted in this way. It was found buried in a muck swamp between three stones and wrapped in deer hide. As these axes weigh from one to three pounds when hung on a fifteen- or eighteen-inch handle they made a very formidable weapon. One blow on the head would be quite sufficient.

The celts are axes but are fastened to the handle quite differently. Instead of being hung between two sticks, they are morticed into one stick. They have no grooves around them at all but are shaped like a pear coming to a point at the top and are wide at the edge. Their edges are mostly highly polished.

The Indians must have raised corn and tobacco. We found a soapstone pipe and also a piece of a pottery pipe. The piece of pottery pipe was beautifully ornamented. It was made like a horn, large at one end and small at the other for the mouth. The soapstone pipe I have here and it is hollowed out for a bowl. They used a reed or bone stem and an open hole is drilled into the bowl. They put the reed into this hole to get to the tobacco.

The mortar which this tribe used is down at Osbrook Point. It is quite shallow and is cut into a big low rock. It is about ten inches in diameter. We have an exceptionally nice pestle which my uncle found many years ago near the river in a field which was always called Plum Bush because of the quantity of wild plums that grew there. Both ends are highly polished. I suppose a great many bushel of corn were ground in this mortar with this pestle. In one deep hole, Bill's wife found three rough hoes packed one on top of the other just as the Indians had laid them away, probably from one year to another. They were almost rotten and were quite thick and clumsy. Bill found a small hoe which is a nice one. It was used as a trowel and they probably dug clams with it. It has a wide blade, highly polished, and is about five inches long.

Of course the Indians made clothes from the skins of animals which they killed or trapped. We find pieces of deer bone ground or worked to a sharp point, which they used as awls in sewing the skins. When we do find them, they are usually broken or cracked. Some, however, are perfect. I have some points sharp as pins. One of the perfect awls is made from a bird bone and is hollow. It is about three inches long and has a long point.

I have four pieces of graphite which the Indians used to paint their faces with. On one side, it is smooth, showing use. Another thing they used was red paint stone. This is a hard stone but makes a red mark when wetted. They made beads out of fish vertebrae. I have seven of those beads and they are quite pretty. They are worked smooth all around the edges, are circular and flat on two sides. There is just a pinpoint of a hole in all fish vertebrae. These pin holes have been enlarged on these beads to admit sinew. The beads are different in size so there must have been quite a string of them at one time.

We know the Indians used nets for catching some of their fish and they also used fish hooks. Bill found a bone fish hook in their winter camp. I have four stones, either grooved or with notches on the sides, that they used to sink their fish nets with. These grooves or notches were to prevent the thongs from slipping off the stone.

Besides the pots, the Indians used the backs of box turtles for dishes. I have a small piece of turtle shell dish which very plainly shows the scraping they gave it to get all the flesh out and to make it clean. We find stones varying in size from the size of your fist to a peck measure which have been hollowed out enough to hold one of these dishes to keep it from tipping over. They set the stone firmly in the ground and put their pots or round bottom dishes on them. We found them near the fire pits.

To break bones, from which they took the marrow, or to do their pounding, the Indians seemed to have special stones in many instances for that purpose. We find smooth hard stones near the fire pits and around the large rocks we find stones with pitted places on them which show hard use from pounding. These are called hammer stones.

Bill always claimed the so-called burying ground was not a burying ground at all. He said the Indians did not bury that way. I finally gave consent to dig into several of these well-defined hollows. In only one did we find anything and that was a small piece of pottery and a yellow jasper stone chip. We found a good shell heap attached to the village of hollows, thereby proving it had been a real Indian village. There were thirty to forty huts in this village set so close together as to hardly admit passage between them.

On Labor Day, Bill made the BIG FIND when he was digging a particularly deep pocket of shells. After he got down about eighteen inches, he came to stones about the size of a twelve quart pail, laid in a line and all exactly the same depth in the ground. There seemed to be shells all around and below them. This indicated they had been placed there by the Indians. Upon removing the stones, the shells led him deeper. He dug down in one end of the shell pit and uncovered an Indian skull in a fine state of preservation. This was due to the shells which completely surrounded it. He then came to the house for me. I went back with him and watched him continue excavating. He uncovered a perfect Indian skeleton.

Buried with the Indian was a perfect box turtle shell dish. It was inverted and placed at the Indian's back. The Indian was in a sitting position but lying down. By that, I mean the knees were drawn up. We estimated this Indian must have been as large as a good-sized man, if not a big man. The cheekbones were so high as to be almost abnormal, with a massive lower jaw, large head, and broad shoulders. He certainly must have been a powerful Indian. Looking from the shell pit around the land he once roamed, I could easily picture him hunting in the woods, always on the lookout for danger of invasion on his hunting grounds from hostile tribes (the Narragansetts across the river, which was the boundary line) or fishing in the cove or river or paddling his canoe around the rocks along the shore for oysters. What a wild, dangerous life he must have had.

Every Indian not belonging to his own tribe when caught on hunting grounds was considered a robber and a murderer. He was a robber because he took food, which was priceless, and he was a murderer because he would have killed anyone who stood in his way because they would have killed him. It was war to the death and no favors asked or given. To go into enemy territory and bring out a deer or other game was a brave thing to do. Each one would want to show his bravery and, of course, this would deplete the others' hunting ground. As a deterrent, the Indians used to capture and then torture the invaders. We know they tortured them for we found ample proof that they did. In one place we found a part of an Indian's back with three or four rib bones on each side and also parts of skull, teeth, and chinbone with small teeth in it, a piece of charred bone, and charcoal around the spot, which to our minds was conclusive proof of a torture by fire. At another place, beside a large stone, we found the lower jaw of a middle-aged Indian in perfect condition. In fact, it looked like a set of false teeth. About three feet away was the battered skull of a very old Indian. We could tell by the teeth being worn down. On the eye socket bone was a flint scratch.

If that big rock could talk, what a tale it would tell! It needs little imagination to picture the scene. They tied or held him across the rock and then danced around, each probably taking a crack at his head with a stone knife or ax. What disposal was made of the rest of these unfortunate captives we do not know for all we found was the battered skull and lower jaw. John Farnsworth of Westerly took photographs of these tortures and also of the burial. The pictures were taken with the dish and everything just as the Indians left it. The dirt only was removed.

A little above the bottom of the pit we found the head of a deer. It had evidently been buried with the Indian to provide the food and was to be eaten from the dish. In all, we found two burials. The second was not surrounded by many shells and so was in a poor state of preservation. Both however were slightly on the side of the hill. Both were buried with the top of the head pointing directly west. The feet of both were pointing toward the east. I add this information for the benefit of those who claim the Indians were always buried facing the rising sun. Mr. Bull and Bill both say this is not so and the way they were found would prove it that way.

The turtle shell dish is in Mr. Bull's collection in Hartford and the skeletons covered again just as the Indians left them.

In the 1930s I had a milk customer by the name of Arthur Chaquette. He was French and came from Saskatchewan, Canada. He was a farmer and a woodsman and had lived near a tribe of Indians all his life. It was very cold in Canada. He said he had seen a horse's ears drop off after being frozen and what hit the ground after you spit would be a piece of ice. He worked with the Indians and played cards with them. One day in a game of poker he bet three dollars against the Indian's shirt and won.

The shirt was made of deerskin. The deer had been killed with a bow and arrow, tanned by the Indian and sewed with sinew. Arthur had a wife and five children and, when he left Canada and came to the United States, he brought the shirt or jacket with him. He did not want to wear it around town as it looked out of place so he just kept it. When I showed him my Indian collection he told me about the jacket and gave it to me. I prize it very highly.

Arthur used to help me here on the farm. He was a fine fellow and became great friends with Jim Anderson and George Chase.

Way back in the late 1700s or early 1800s, there was an Indian worked here by the name of Garner. There is a stone bridge down on the marsh which was always called Garner's Bridge. I asked Uncle John one day why it was called that and then he told me about Garner. Garner built the bridge. He used three large flat stones for the top. This bridge has stood there for many years and must have been well built to do it. Heavy loads of hay, wood, etc., have been carted over it and it is still good and sturdy.

Now Garner lived here in the house and had a dugout canoe which he kept down to the river, tied to the river bank. I do not know what became of the canoe but the paddle he used and which he made himself, of course, he kept here in the house so no one could use his boat without his knowing about it. When Garner went away he left the paddle here and never came back for it. It is still here in my Indian collection.

John Davis, VII, Clad in Indian Costume

Twelve-year-old John Whitman Davis displays an paddle from his father's collection of Indian artifacts. The family believed it to be the property of an Indian known as Garner, who lived in the homestead. The photograph appeared in the New London Day *on February 27, 1937.*

CHAPTER 10

MORE ABOUT ELLERY CRUMB

Ellery liked cider and would often come to visit Uncle John. He would stay and stay and talk about mostly nothing until Uncle, who like everyone knew what he wanted, would say, "Would you like a glass of cider, Ellery?" Ellery would always say, "Well, I wouldn't mind, Uncle John," and then he would smile all over.

Uncle would give him a glass or two of cider and then Ellery would leave, saying he guessed he would go out and get a woodchuck. He had a good fox hound, one which would follow a fox all day if necessary. He hunted about every weekend, on Saturday. Between Wolcott Main of Wequetequock and Uncle, Ellery got plenty of cider but both were careful not to give him too much to drink at one time. Ellery drove a car and they didn't want to get him into trouble with it. When he would show up at Wolcott's, Wolk would ask him if he had been over to John's and would also analyze his condition. If Ellery's eyes were a little watery, etc., Wolcott would talk with him about an hour, then allow him one glass. In that way Ellery was well taken care of. Wolcott figured that if he waited an hour or more, some of that which Uncle had given him would wear off and he wouldn't have to refuse him altogether.

Sometime Ellery would walk down to the farm on Sundays and he would visit with Uncle Tom Burrell. Tom always had cider on hand for himself and company and

Ellery was of course invited to drink, which he always did. Not having a car to drive at such times, Tom would let him drink all he wanted, which was plenty.

Now there are different kinds of "drunks." When people become intoxicated to the point where they more or less lose their senses they are affected in different ways. There is the resentful or "quarrelsome jag." Such people want to fight. Then there is the "laughing jag." Everything that ordinarily wouldn't even cause them to smile suddenly becomes hilariously funny and they just can't stop laughing. These people are good companions, harmless and amusing. They get along with everybody. Then there is the "crying jag." It comes on slowly; they begin to consider themselves as having been wronged at some time or other. The more they drink, the more sympathy they have for themselves until they can't bear it any longer and begin to cry.

Now, Tom's jags were always of the laughing kind and he had one every weekend. He would come to work on Monday morning only about half over it and what fun we would have all day. I always looked forward to Monday and greeting Tom. If his condition was such, I would say, "Good morning, Tom, you're drunk again." He would eye me owlishly for a moment, then he would say, "No, sir, this is the same old drunk, only a little worse." Then how we both would laugh. That kept up most all day. Tom was so good-natured.

One Monday morning he came over to work and before I could question him about being drunk he began to laugh. "Boy," he said, "I got something to tell you. You know Ellery Crumb?" The question was more a statement than a question, for of course I did. "Well," said Tom, "he was over to the house yesterday and we had a little cider, maybe more than a little probably." He stopped and thought a bit. "Well, maybe five or six glasses apiece. I guess about that. Well, anyway, Ellery got a crying jag on. It seems that his son, Merle, was working in some small store in town. He had worked there for quite some time but one Saturday he came home to dinner looking sad and depressed, was gloomy, didn't eat much dinner. Ellery saw the boy was upset about something or other and inquired what was troubling him. Tom said it went like this:

"Well, Father," Merle said to Ellery, "I think I am going to get fired tonight. Things haven't been going just right at the store and I am pretty sure to be discharged tonight."

"Now boy,' Ellery said, 'Don't let them fire you. If you do you can't get a recommendation from them for another job. What you should do is quit before they can fire you, then you will have left them of your own accord. They can't discharge you because you won't be working for them and when you seek another job, you can say that you got through yourself because you didn't like it there. What time do you get off work tonight?"

"I get through at six o'clock," said Merle.

"All right," Ellery said. "You go to the desk at a quarter to six and tell them that you are all through, that they will have to get somebody else Monday morning, and ask for your money. Then I think everything will be all right. In that way we can outsmart them and you will not have been discharged."

That evening about six o'clock Merle came home. He looked quite downhearted and sober, not at all cheerful as Ellery thought he would.

"Well, boy," Ellery asked, "Did you quit at quarter to six tonight?"

"No, Father," Merle replied. "They fired me at half past five."

Tom said Ellery put his head down on the table and cried harder than ever. There was no justice in the world and everything was against him. Of that he was sure.

CHAPTER 11

TWO FOR FIVE

Cap was quite a boy, always out for fun and a good time.

Now there was a certain woman in town who was married to a half-witted fellow named Bennie. Bennie couldn't work much, if any at all, so his wife had to do the supporting. She did this in various ways.

One night there was no bread for supper, so she went out looking for money to buy some with. Bread at that time was a nickel a loaf. She met a couple of fellows who, to see just how cheaply she would work, offered her five cents for the two of them. She accepted and was thereafter known in that circle of society as "two for five."

Cap had a friend who came to town one time for a short stay. He wanted a girl companion and, knowing Cap was well acquainted around town, asked him if he could help him out.

Knowing "two for five" was always available, Cap said he would do what he could for him and let him know. The fellow insisted, however, that it would all have to be done in the dark as he didn't want to be recognized at any time, either now or in the future. Cap explained it all out to "two for five," who readily agreed, saying she didn't mind the dark at all and would meet him anywhere, anytime.

Cap set the date to be down at the end of a lane by the river. She was to take the trolley and he gave her a twenty-five cent piece for carfare.

The evening of the date, Cap was in the pool room when in walked his friend. Cap asked him how he made out and the fellow said, "All right, but did you pay her? She would not take any money from me."

Cap said she must have accepted the quarter he gave her for carfare as full payment. Both agreed she was a good honest woman not to overcharge. The fellow said there was only one thing he didn't like. She had on long-legged rubber boots and he nearly froze his behind.

How Cap did laugh.

CHAPTER 12

SMITH AND THE PIG

A man I will call Henry Smith came from Ledyard, Connecticut, about 1915 and bought a small farm here in Lower Pawcatuck on which he raised vegetables for a living. He was a hard worker and taught me a bit about that phase of farming.

In the 1930's, another man came from Ledyard I'll call Johnson and he also bought a small farm, adjoining Smith's. Johnson had no wife or family, only a small dog for a companion. Smith and Johnson got along well enough for a while, then they had a difference of opinion that led to their not speaking to each other. I heard both sides of the story from each of them and I guess they were both to blame.

One day, I was visiting Smith and somehow the name of Johnson came up and Smith told me this story about his father and Johnson's father. It seems that Mr. Smith's father bought a pig from Mr. Johnson's father at a certain price per pound which both agreed on. Getting up early one morning, Mr. Smith went over to Mr. Johnson's farm to get his pig and take him home. Arriving at Mr. Johnson's house, he found that Mr. Johnson as yet hadn't gotten up. Mr. Smith pounded on the door several times before Mr. Johnson opened a window and called down to see who was there.

Mr. Smith said it was he and he had come to get his pig. Mr. Johnson said he would be right down and, after a while, he opened the door and asked Mr. Smith to come in while he put on his shoes. Mr. Smith came in and sat down to wait for Mr. Johnson to finish dressing. Mr. Johnson made no effort to put on his shoes on and kept up a conversation about everything in general and nothing in particular. No mention about the pig at all.

Suddenly, the pigs out in the pen began to squeal and grunt in a loud manner. Mr. Smith looked out the window and saw Mr. Johnson's wife there feeding the pigs, putting the pails of feed right to them and they were eating greedily. Mr. Johnson had been stalling Mr. Smith so his wife could feed the pigs and make them heavier when they were put on the scales. Mr. Smith immediately went to the pen, jumped over the fence and grabbed the pig he wanted and pulled it away from the trough so it couldn't eat any more.

Mr. Johnson by this time had his shoes on. He wanted the pig to eat more, said it wouldn't hurt him. Mr. Smith objected, saying he was paying a good price for the pig and didn't intend to pay that price for swill. If the pig ate any more, he just wouldn't take it at all. Mr. Johnson finally agreed and they got the pig out of the pen and into the barn where there was a set of steelyards (balances).

Making a sling out of a rope, which went under the pig, they hoisted it up off the ground and slipped the rope on the hook of the balances. They then pushed the weight or pee along the arm of the balances and, when the arm was straight across, or level, that would be the weight marked on the arm, where the pee rested.

The arm finally came level and they looked closely at the mark to see what the weight was. Just then the arm went down a bit, just a little off balance. They both looked to see what had changed the weight a few ounces and found the pig had just made manure. Mr. Smith quickly gathered this up with both hands and laid in on the pig's back. The arm returned to level and Mr. Smith said, "There is your weight, neighbor. Right there, neighbor, right there."

Johnson concluded the story and, looking up into my face, said "Don't you think that was pretty small of him to do that?"

I could only agree that it was.

CHAPTER 13

HOGS

Hogs were or are the most important farm product. On this farm, they still are and the meat is cured and smoked just as it was two hundred years ago.

We just butchered two hogs. One weighed 265 pounds and the other, 225 pounds. This is just about the right weight to make very good cuts, nice-sized bacon and pork chops. There are the front shoulder hams, the hind or round hams, six strips of bacon per hog, the jowls or lower jaws, the leaf for lard, the legs for boiling, and the trimmings for sausage. Then there is the fat pork from the back which is salted in crock jars for beans, chowders, etc. We plan to salt fifty pieces which gives us one piece a week for one year, from fall to fall. We salted the pork yesterday and Sally and I made thirty-two pounds of sausage. This and the pork chops will go into the freezer, thirty-five pounds of chops.

Before we had the freezer, we would take a crock jar, put a layer of sausage meat all fixed about four inches thick in the bottom then pour a thin layer of lard one inch thick over the sausage and then a layer of meat and so on until the jar was full or you had used up all the meat. The last layer was lard. This was kept down in the cellar where it was cool and it preserved well.

The bacon and ham were put in a brine, then taken to the smoke house to be smoked. The 1938 hurricane destroyed our old smoke house so we built a new one. It is small, with a dug fire hole in the ground, partly covered with flat stones. It holds about or a little more than one half bushel corn cobs and about one half bushel hardwood chips from the wood pile. The cobs are placed in first, then two or three quarts of burning coals from the kitchen stove are covered with some of the cobs, then the chips on top of that, then some sawdust to kill the blaze. The object is to make it smoke and not blaze as the blaze will make it too hot and might cook the meat somewhat or at least soften it so the that strings will tear out. It has to be watched carefully and more sawdust and sometimes water added.

One time when we had a good smoke going and the smoke was pouring out from the cracks between the boards, a car drove in the yard and a man ran up to the door and knocked loudly on it. I answered his knock and when I opened the door, he exclaimed excitedly, "Do you know your toilet is on fire? I saw it from the road."

Seeing a chance for a joke, I said, "We are all in the house. There is nobody in it, so let it go."

He looked at me as though he knew I was crazy but didn't know just what he should do about it, fight or run. He kept backing away and I followed him outdoors. Pointing to the smoke house I asked if that was it. Yes, he told me and then asked if I wanted to lose it.

No, I replied and then I explained to him and how he did laugh. "Well," he said, "I thought I was doing you a favor." "You were," I told him. "And thank you for being so kind. Good luck to you, sir, and thanks again." He drove off laughing. I bet he told that one around. I know I did. When things like this happen, it leads me to believe that the whole world isn't bad, just a small part of it.

A word as to the time to butcher. Many people will ridicule this but I go by the moon. Kill your hogs on a rising moon, not on a declining one. The pork will be sweet and good on a rising moon but is not to be on a declining moon. I don't know why this is so but it has proved to be this way with me.

This is not entirely my own idea. When I was young I was engaged by a neighbor to dress off his hog for him. I picked the day on which I was going to kill one for myself. Thinking I would do the both of them together and save a heating of water, I notified him that I was ready. He objected, saying the moon was wrong for butchering. I laughed at his foolish idea and went ahead and killed my hog. To my surprise, the meat was strong, not but what is all right to use, but it just wasn't as sweet as it should be. When the moon was on the rise, I killed his hog. He asked me how mine turned out and I told him. He said, "You should butcher on the rising moon and your pork will be sweet. It you don't, it will not be so good." I knew his hog was good because I took particular pains to find out. So now I go by the moon with good results.

I also go by the moon when planting garden seeds. Whit and I have both observed the results of planting both ways and we have decided to always plant when the moon is on the rise. It is quite sure to storm three days before, on, or three days after, the full of the moon. If you don't believe this, check it out and see. I think you will be surprised how often it comes out that way.

I am reminded of a poem about the moon:

> *He stood on the bridge at midnight*
> *Drunk as a son of a gun*
> *Two moons rose over the city*
> *When there should have only been one.*

It has been the custom of this farm for two hundred years to butcher the hogs around November 10 or so, and a beef, either a bull or a cow which has passed its usefulness for milking, about January 10. This gave a supply of fresh meat most of the winter.

The hams of the beef were cut out and brined same as the pork hams, in the same brine. Then smoked. They would be given four or five smokes. A smoke was supposed to go all day. Then they were kept for dried beef gravy. Some would be eaten as steak before they became hard. They would get hard on the outside but remain soft on the inside and would keep for years just hung up in the corn crib.

All hams and bacon were enclosed with a paper bag, the mouth of which was tied tightly around the string from which they were suspended. This kept the flies away from the meat. Now of course all meat goes into the freezer, both fresh and cured. Much of the beef was just left in the brine. This was corned beef and would keep in that way most of the summer. Of course, the barrel of brine was down in the cellar where it is cool.

CHAPTER 14

HORSES AND CATTLE

During the 1930's I used to visit the Connecticut State College at Storrs. They had some nice Percheron horses which they worked about the college farm, haying, hauling gravel, etc. The horses would weigh one ton or more, and they only charged $15 for the service of their stallion.

I did not have a mare to breed so I thought I would buy me one, take her up there, breed her for $15 and get a good big colt and I would be in business. I asked a horse dealer, or I thought he was, where I could get such an animal. He said he knew of two or three and would go with me to see them.

We went off into the wilds of Central Village or somewhere and stopped at a good-sized farm. Yes, he had a mare which he would sell. He had been delivering his milk on a route with her but was going to change to a truck. The price was $125. We got him down to $110 and I bought the mare. I think my friend got $10 and the owner got $100.

Anyway, I hired a truck to bring her down and rode home with my friend. When we unloaded her, he said to me, "Do you know anything about this horse?" I said, "No." "Well," he said, "Look out you don't get hurt with her. She is about as mean a one as I ever saw, she will not work double and not too good single either." I thanked him for telling me and he left.

She was a peculiar looking mare, one-third head (she had an awfully big head), one-third body and one-third rump. I guess she would weigh around fourteen or fifteen hundred pounds. I thought to myself, I guess you have got it.

John Lawrence Davis and one of his horses, probably Josie, which he taught tricks. Below, he does a handstand on horseback.

When I fed her grain the next morning, I knew I had it. I dumped four quarts of horsefeed in her manger and she tried to bite me. She took the whole four quarts in one mouthful. Her ears were lapped back tight to her head and her eyes just glared at me. Now I did something then which I shouldn't have done and which I never did do again. She made me angry and I went around the stable and straight for her stall. I guess she was so surprised at my action that for a moment she did nothing at all.

Then she woke up fast. She began by throwing her weight against me, trying to crowd me against the side of the stall. Remember she weighed about fourteen hundred pounds. I jumped into the corner of the stall close to the manger by her head. She couldn't crowd me there, but she did her best. When she backed up to bite me I grabbed her nose with my left hand and shut off her wind. This caused her mouth to open for air. I caught her tongue with my right hand and hung on tight to it, pulling it between her teeth. If she had tried to close her jaws, then she would have bitten her own tongue off.

I managed to hold her till she quieted down, then I let her go and got out of the stall. As I turned by the end of the stall partition, something went past the back of my head. It was her heels, both of them. She was a good one!

I knew I had been taken but I was determined to put her to work. I got a clothesline rope, made a loop to fit around her lower jaw and climbed into her manger from in front. She backed off but I pulled her up to me and got the rope in her mouth, making some twists around her head, back of the ears. I now had a powerful bridle which, when I jerked it hard, punished her severely. She gave up to this quite a bit or at least so I could harness her.

I worked this mare for six weeks double but how she would kick when hitched beside another horse. She wouldn't kick at the horse, just kicked, and she was powerful. She would pull the whole load and the other horse, too. The only way I could handle her at stall was with the war bridle. I kept it on all the time.

Six weeks was enough for me. I was away mornings with milk and could only work afternoons. I wouldn't let the help try to drive her as they might get hurt so I decided to get rid of her. But where? Who would take such a thing as she? She would kill anybody. A veterinarian told me her ovaries were diseased and there was no cure.

There was a horse dealer in town who brought in a carload a week from the West. He was honest and a good man. I went to see him and told him what I had. His name was Ledyard Anthony and he said if I could get the mare to his barn by three o'clock that afternoon he could get her trucked to an auction in Providence to be sold at the end of a halter. This meant that no guarantee of any sort went with her. I got her there and never saw her again or ever want to.

Two or three days later, I saw Ledyard and asked how he made out. He said all right, she brought $55 and went to a logging camp somewhere or the other. He asked me if I wanted a good brood mare, said he had a good one, safe in foal. She was bred and he didn't know it when he bought her in the West. No one wanted a mare in foal as they couldn't work her so much. He showed me his book where he paid $150 her and said he would sell her to me for that figure and allow me $50 for my mare. I took her, of course. She foaled a dead mule colt but I bred her to one of the big horses at Storrs and got a nice colt. She was a good tough mare and I kept her as long as she lived, which was a good old age.

I have lots of experience with horses and colts and have broken about twenty-five or more, maybe thirty. All did well. I went by some horse-breaking books which I bought when I was about sixteen years old. They were great stuff, Jesse Beery's Horse-Breaking Course.

They told me at Storrs they would sell me a stallion colt, then I wouldn't have to bring my mare way up there to be bred each time. I did as they suggested and purchased a six-month-old colt named Roy. I took in service fees enough to pay for him, $125 and then some. He was quite a horse, excitable and nervous, but he and I got along all right. I broke him so a kid could drive him, took him to the North Stonington Fair and all around. I don't know what the matter was with him but when he was eight years old he died. I then brought another stallion from Storrs. He had heart trouble and died as a four-year-old.

When Storrs sold out all their Percherons I bought a beautiful gray three-year-old mare. I had a three-year-old mare I had raised myself so thought the two of them would make a good team as they were of the same color and size.

I had broken mine and she was very reliable and good. The other was broken also, they said, and could be put right to work. I thought she could stand a little more breaking, however, and so I put her through more training. She was coming along very well and then came a day of hitching her up to wagon.

I had a four-wheel buggy and we took her down in the meadow below the house, where we could have plenty of room. It was level. I hitch all my colts down there the first time. We put her in the shafts, turned her to the right and left, stopped and started her and she worked fine. This mare is just as they said she was at Storrs, I thought, she is going good.

We then drove her up the house over the stony lane and she never bothered at all. It was about four o'clock and I thought I would drive her out on the highway and go for a ride. I sent Whit in to ask his mother if she would like to ride behind our beautiful purebred colt on its first drive. He said Sally was lying down upstairs and would have to dress and get ready. I said, "Never mind, it's late and I will go alone, we'll take her some other time."

I spoke to the mare, she started up and we went around the house and started down the road. Suddenly, she tightened up and I stopped her with the command, "Whoa," and a jerk on the lines. She soon relaxed and we started on. I couldn't figure out why she had tightened up. We proceeded about five hundred feet down the road when she did it again. Again I stopped her saying, "Whoa," and giving a pull on the lines. Again she relaxed and I started her up.

We started up all right; she made a leap about twenty-five feet long, the front wheels came off the ground two feet, and she acted panic-stricken. On a dead run we headed for a stone wall about three hundred feet away. I pulled and sawed on the lines as hard as I could but they might have been tied to a tree for all the good it did. It seemed as though her head was down against her chest, I pulled so hard on the bit. She seemed insensible to everything but running but she was doing a good job of that, just crazy running.

When we were halfway to the wall I did some fast thinking. I knew I couldn't stop her or steer her away from the wall and I didn't want to be in the wagon when it hit. There would be a terrible crash. Either she would go over the wall or against it. Whichever way it was, it wasn't going to be fun. I decided to leave the wagon. I stood up, still pulling on the lines with all my might. Leaning over the side I jumped out and began running before my feet touched the ground. The wagon flew past me. Freed of all restraint, the mare leaped the wall, smashing the wagon into kindling wood, breaking the harness all to pieces, and freeing her. She galloped across the lot and down to the barn where Whit was doing chores. He caught her and put her in her stall. She did not get hurt in the least.

When I landed, I sprained my ankle. As the wagon passed me, the spokes of the hind wheel connected with my left elbow and raised a knot on it which I can feel to the present day. I limped back to the barn to see how the mare was and told Whit what happened. He said how fortunate it was that Sally hadn't been there with me on that ride. Had she been ready in time, she and I both would have hit that wall together as I wouldn't have jumped and left her alone in the wagon. It was a close call.

Whit and I took stock of the situation and both firmly agreed that no horse in the future would be driven its first few times without the safety rope being on. The safety rope is sometimes called the running W and is used in the West on broncos. It is rigged so as to trip the horse by pulling its front legs up. The horse then has to fall on its knees. It is very effective and shows the horse you can control him no matter what.

My ankle hurt so badly the next morning that I went to the doctor about it. He used his vibrator on the sore spot and then put on small bandage with a piece of cloth for a pad. It felt so good when he finished I could feel no pain at all. He was a darn good doctor.

I came home, changed my clothes, went out to the barn and called for everybody to come on the run. We took the mare out, got another harness and rigged up the running W. We drove her back to where she had begun to run away, no wagon this time. She thought she could try to get away again and tried to but the W did its work as it was supposed to do. She landed on her nose. She fought the rope for a while then pretty much gave up.

I worked her all summer but had to use the W when she was in the horse rake. The rake made a noise she didn't like when it tripped to release the hay and she would jump a little. She was always looking for something to be afraid of and could usually find it soon enough.

Now here is something else. When I examined her for injuries after the smash-up, I discovered a four- or five-inch scar back of her left foreleg. I put two and two together and figured she had been in a ruckus before I got her.

Sometime later I was up at Storrs and I mentioned the gray mare to them. Did she ever try to run away up here, I asked. Oh, well she just went down the lane and stopped by the church, it wasn't much, they said. Wasn't much, I thought. It was enough to nearly kill my wife.

A horse that once runs away will always be a hazard until it has had a lot of subjective treatment over a period of several months. I didn't tell them of the scrape I had with her because that would seem like a complaint. I bought her, paid for her. She was my horse and I was responsible for her actions. However, they should have told about it and then I would have been on my guard. That scar back of her leg spoke for itself.

About five days after I had been to the doctor about my ankle I got out of bed one morning and it pained me so I could hardly walk. I hobbled around and did my chores, ate breakfast, then called up the doctor on the phone. I told him how lame I was and asked what I should do about it. "Is the bandage on?" he asked. No, I said. Where is it, he wanted to know. "I guess it came off in bed," I replied. "Get it and put it on and be sure that little piece of cloth is on under it," he said. "That little piece of cloth has cocaine on it." I did as he said and the pain stopped. He was a good doctor.

I have always had a saddle horse ever since I was three years old. My Uncle John brought me a six-month-old Shetland stallion when I was three years old. I named the pony Jack Farmer and we grew up together. My father broke him to cart after I broke him to ride. I rode him bareback as I had no saddle small enough to fit him.

When I did get a saddle, Father and Uncle saw to it that the stirrups were covered as I could only put my toes in them. That was so that, if I was thrown, my foot wouldn't get caught in the stirrup and I wouldn't be dragged on the ground beside the horse. An accident of this kind had happened in the neighborhood when they were boys. A boy twelve or thirteen years old was riding a horse at a gallop from this direction toward the Lower Pawcatuck Schoolhouse at Four Corners. He expected the horse would go straight across toward Wequetequock down Mary Hall Lane. The boy, caught off balance, pitched over to the left side of the horse and his foot caught in the stirrup. The horse ran all the way to the river and when it was caught, the boy was dead.

Cowboys ride with open stirrups but they also wear high-heeled boots so the boot cannot go through the stirrup. If they are thrown then, they will not be caught.

Our cow pasture was a mile from the house and Uncle used to give me five cents a night to bring the cows home with my pony. The little fellow soon became very expert in driving them. If a cow was slow and lagged behind he would lop his ears, run up and bite her on the rump. He was a good pony.

When I grew too big to ride him I had a saddle horse which I traded for with a Mr. Browning. He lived on a farm over by the Road Church. She was a sorrel in color. Her name was Josie with both hind feet and ankles white. She would drive as well as ride and was pretty and stylish. I used to chew a small piece of ginger root until it was moist, then lift her tail and insert it in her rectum. Then I would saddle her up and go for a ride uptown. How she would keep her tail raised. Some class! Wow!

I taught her to say "yes" by nodding her head and "no" by shaking it. Also to count by pawing the required number of times I wished her to. I also taught her to high step like a circus horse. I used to show her off a lot.

I had gotten Professor Jesse Berry's mail course in horsemanship and soon I was breaking colts and horses for others in this area. I received $25 at first, then went to $35. This was a small fortune to me. It took from three to four weeks per colt, training every day from one to three hours. Before driving them on the road much I would take them to Sam Bailey's Blacksmith Shop on Coggswell Street to have them shod. After the shoes were nailed on by George Pickering, a wonderful horseshoer, the colt would shake and stamp his foot to get the shoes off. I suppose it felt funny to have something stuck to the bottom of his feet.

I remember one time I rode Josie to the shop to have her shoes changed. I just about made the shop before the thunderstorm broke. It rained hard and thundered and lightninged severely for nearly one hour. Upon arriving home I found the house had been struck by lightning. It came in on the telephone wires across the desk where I am writing this. My sister had just gotten up from the desk and gone upstairs to close a window. It went through the partition into the kitchen and set the face towels hanging on a rack on fire. Needless to say, we now keep away from the telephone during a thunderstorm.

That reminds me of another incident which occurred in a July. In the afternoon, I was picking stringbeans in the garden

(I take this from my Farm Diary). In the west, there had been dull mutterings and rumblings of thunder all afternoon. At four o'clock I could see the rain coming so left off picking and came to the house. It soon began to rain and rained until 6:30 p.m. We then went to the barn to milk. When we had finished milking it hadn't cleared off but the rain had let up. There were two mares, with their colts, two other horses, and a year-old colt to turn to pasture for the night. We had mowed the North Lot and the second growth, called afterfeed or rowen, was making good pasture for them. We turned them out and put up the bars. They were safe and on good feed for the night.

The next day was Saturday and, as it happened, we weren't going to use the team until Monday so we wouldn't go for them in the morning as usual. Otherwise, they would have been put in the barn and fed before going to work. About ten o'clock, a neighbor, Mrs. Williams, telephoned that she could see a dead horse from her window over in the North Lot. We went to investigate and sure enough it was one of the mares with a young colt. The colt was standing beside its dead mother. We looked for the other horses and saw the other mare with her little colt on the other side of the lot, down by the woods. She was dead too. Her colt was walking around nearby. This meadow contains six acres and the mares were on opposite sides of the lot. They must have been killed by lightning. The other horses were okay.

Now I know that many people do not believe in a witch stick. A witch stick is a forked stick, usually of wild cherry or willow. One prong is held in each hand and the user walks around until he comes to an underground vein of water. Then the fork is supposed to dip down and point to the vein. With some people it doesn't work, no matter how hard they try to follow directions given them by someone for whom it does work. It always works to perfection for me, my son, and my grandson. We never dig a well or open up a dry water hole with a bulldozer unless we locate the vein first.

Three or four years ago we had a dry spell and an old water hole had completely dried up. The soil in it was dry and cracked from the heat of the sun. I had given it up but Whit wanted to try to get water there and had Dudley Wheeler come down with his tractor bucket loader to dig. The hole was about thirty feet across. They started on one side and dug six or seven feet down. The bottom of the hole was just a little cold and damp. Dud wanted to know should he continue or quit as it was noontime. Whit said to try it after dinner.

They went back and this time Whit took a willow witch stick. He tried it over the hole they had made and it showed nothing. He then tried it at different places and found one where there was a strong pull on the stick. Dig there, he said. Dud had his son with him and they both laughed but Dud moved his rig and began to dig. In less than ten minutes and down about three and a half foot he nearly got stuck, the water came in so fast. Young Dud could hardly believe his eyes. He asked Whit to show him how to work the stick. Whit did and young Wheeler worked it fine. We then went to another dry water hole and Dud used his stick to locate the vein. He hit it right on the nose, right where, years ago, a half barrel had been sunk in the ground to keep the sides from filling in the hole by cattle drinking there. How pleased he was, he couldn't get over it.

Now to get back to the two dead mares:

I wondered if they had both been struck by the same bolt of lightning or two separate ones. I took a forked stick of wild cherry, held it in the correct position and walked around the mare at the top of the hill. The stick turned down. She lay right in the middle of fifteen-foot-wide vein of water. I then traced the vein by using the witch stick all the way down the hill to where the other mare was. She too lay on the vein. The bolt of lightning had followed that underground vein of water to wherever it went and had killed both mares as they happened to be standing on it. I think that is why we are told not to go out in an open lot or stand under a tree during a thunderstorm. There are veins of water in the open lot and the trees' roots branch out in the ground searching for water for the tree to live.

Later on, I had another saddle mare which I bought by mail from Kentucky. She was of the American Saddle Horse breed and I don't think much of them. They are high-headed and foolish. This one's bad habit was to shy at everything she saw along the road and she saw plenty. She was good and fast and strong and I used her all her life.

We would get to the pasture looking for calves which would be hidden by their mothers so they could not be found. A cow's instinct is to hide her calf. Probably goes back to the days of the wolves. This mare would point them out to me by pricking up her ears and looking intently into the thick bushes. I could tell by her actions that there was something there and it was most always a calf. I would tie her to a bush, grab the calf before he became frightened and lift him up across her shoulders. Then I would mount and we would bring the calf to the barn where its mother was, she having come home with the other cows.

A farm boy is trained through necessity to observe things which have a profound bearing on his daily life, such as a hen cackling off in the weeds. She has a nest there and you should look for eggs. Sheep bleating, probably one or two have jumped out of the lot. They must be put back and the fence repaired. A flock of hens making a peculiar noise and running for cover, a hawk is after them. A thumping in the barn, probably a horse is loose and fighting the others. I could go on and on.

Here is where my farm training came in one day and saved me from something that was very serious. After finishing my milk route I would got to the grocery store for my groceries on the way home. It was Groppelli's store on the corner of Palmer and Prospect Streets in Pawcatuck. There were tenement houses all around there and numerous children of all ages. This particular day I parked the old big Buick I was using to deliver milk in front of such a house, where there were eight or ten children, from three to ten years old. They were playing on the doorstep.

I went into the store, made my purchases and came back to my car. I got in and started the motor. It was a standard shift and as I was about to throw in the clutch I glanced at the kids on the doorstep. Something was wrong. They seemed excited about something and were looking at the front of my car. They weren't relaxed as they had been when I went to the store. To see what apparently upset them I got out of the car and walked around in front. Something was wrong, all right. There sat a kid not four years old right on my front bumper. My training to pay attention to the unusual was what saved the kid and me too. Boy, that was a close one!

When the stallion Roy died at eight years of age, he left a number of colts in this area which he had sired. I had to replace him as he had been one of a team which I was working regularly. I thought it would be nice to get one of his colts if I could. So I went to a man up in Ledyard who I knew had raised three from him. I called at his house and was told he was down in the woods hauling logs to go to the sawmill. I followed directions and soon found him. He was working a team, a mare and her billy colt. The colt was well broken and I could see by the way she worked she was just what I wanted. The fellow said he would sell her as his other two colts were working well too. The price was $150. I considered that cheap enough as it was a mare and I could breed her sometime and get it all back. He said he would bring her over the next day for me, which he did. He led her behind a wagon and drove one of his other horses. I gave him a check for $150, thanked him and he took his leave. I led my new mare into the barn, tied her in a stall and went back to woodpile where I had been splitting wood.

The gray mare which I had bought from Ledyard Anthony, and was kind and gentle, was tied in the stall next to my new mare. The stall partition between was stoutly made of two-inch oak plank. I heard a thump and then more thumps. The pounding became a racket so loud I hurried to investigate. I went into the barn and, believe it or not, that partition was kicked down level with the floor.

Dolly, the Anthony mare, was as far away from the new horse as she could get and apparently afraid for her life. The new mare had cleaned out the stable and she hadn't been on the farm ten minutes. I applied several choice swear words at the new addition to my horse stable and also to her former owner. Then I retrieved Dolly from her dangerous position. I took Kitty, the new mare, out of the stable and tied her to a tree. As soon as I removed Dolly, Kitty quieted down and was perfectly tractable. Jim Anderson and I went to work repairing the stall. It was flat, the two-inch planks lying in every direction. We worked all afternoon and finally got it replaced, good and strong.

I then led Kitty back into it again to see what would happen. Nothing did, she was perfectly happy. I then put Dolly back and it started all over again. Kitty meant business, I could see that. So I moved Dolly another stall over, leaving an empty one between them. This seemed to satisfy Kitty so much, she stopped kicking. Everything was quiet from then on.

The next day, we harnessed Kitty beside another horse and she didn't like it one bit. Whenever the other horse touched her she would resent it by biting or kicking, not enough to put up an out-and-out fight but just enough to be annoying. Sometime later, about four or five days, I called on Ledyard Anthony and was telling him about it. I said I couldn't understand it as I saw her working double myself and she was all right.

Ledyard looked at me and said, "You know, Davis, they must be pretty smart up there in Ledyard. That mare will work double only with her own mother and that was the horse she was working with that day you saw them. They delivered her to you and came right up here and bought another horse that same day and used your check to pay for it. The trouble in the barn is because they had a stud colt that kept tearing and fighting this mare over a low partition. That got her so bad she won't let another horse come near her. What you can do about it, I don't know, but that is the story."

"Thank you, Ledyard." I said. "Thank you very much for telling me. There is going to be something done about it and don't you think there isn't. But I will never complain."

Ledyard used to say the word SMART in different ways. If someone tried to cheat him, he would say they tried to get smart. If he protected himself successfully while they thought they were cheating him, he would say they were too smart. If something was done of which he approved he would say that that was smart.

I was angry about this deal and I vowed on the way home that I would get Kitty over her trouble. She was only four years old and, therefore just a colt. I broke colts and I made up my mind I would train this one, bad as she was. I arrived home and, without changing my clothes, I went straight for the horse stable. Jim was there and I told him to lead Kitty out with just the halter on. He did and I held her. Bring out Dolly, I said.

We led them both together, slowly, until their noses touched. This is the test of being friendly between two horses. If they want to fight, they will then. These two mares showed no indication of fighting. Kitty wasn't too friendly but she submitted to it. Jim then led them around, side by side, for five minutes and nothing happened.

Harness them together, I said. Jim did and immediately the fight was on. "Whoa," I said. "Put an open bridle on Kitty and, if that don't work, we will have to teach her to submit to having another horse beside her. It will have to be the war bridle." Jim changed the bridle, we started the team and, to our great surprise, Kitty was as calm as could be. We drove them around and never had any more trouble at all. As soon as Kitty felt another horse touch her which she couldn't see, she protected herself by kicking it. When she could see the other horse and knew the animal to be friendly, then she wasn't afraid.

I worked Kitty with no more trouble all her life, bred her and raised colts from her. She turned out to be one of the best. I saw Ledyard a while after and during our conversation he asked me what I did about the mare I bought in Ledyard. Would she work or did I have to get rid of her, he asked. I told him about the open bridle and he laughed and seemed pleased.

"You were very smart," he said. "These fellows up there weren't as smart as they thought they were." I considered this a great compliment coming as it did from Ledyard Anthony.

One day, six months after I bought Kitty, I was working in the horse stable when I heard voices outside. A man with a seven- or eight-year-old child came into the barn. "Hello there," he said. "How are you?" Good, I replied, how are you? It was the fellow from whom I had bought Kitty.

"Have you got the mare I sold you?" he asked. Sure, I said, she is right here. "Want to see her?" I asked.

He walked down to her stall and told the child to stand back, not too close to the stall, out of the way. She might kick, he said. "Kick?" I said and I seemed surprised. "She won't kick. Whatever gave you that idea?"

I walked in beside her and she was perfectly relaxed with her ears pricked up to see what I wanted. I patted her on the shoulder, ran my hand down over her rump and picked up her hind leg. I stepped hard on the bottom of her foot, then set it down again.

"She doesn't kick," I said. "She is one of the best and I thank you for selling me such a nice horse."

Kitty had gotten used to Dolly and they were tied together in adjoining stalls. I could see he noticed this too. He talked a while, then left. I could see I had given him something to think about.

One day I was coming home from town on Josie, my trick mare. We were just jogging along slowly. It was a hot day and I was letting her take her time. The roads were all dirt in those days, some parts of them would be quite sandy, others hard clay. In the spring, that clay could be awfully muddy. As we approached a sandy section Josie put her ears forward and looked hard at something in the road. I looked to see what had aroused her interest.

It was a snake, all coiled up into a circle, a little bigger than a coffee cup. Its head was sticking out of the coil about four inches and it would run out its tongue at us. I looked for something to kill it with but saw nothing suitable. We passed by when I thought of something. I stopped Josie, turned her around and walked her back toward the snake which was still coiled as we had left it. When about ten feet away from it, I gave her the signal to high step. She immediately went into her act, lifting one foot high off the ground, then the other, and advancing a step each time. I guided her toward the coiled snake and, when over it, she brought her iron-shod hoof down squarely on the top of the coil, smacking the snake flatter than a pancake. I patted her neck and told her what a good horse she was. She seemed to enjoy it.

I got Josie in trade for a work colt I had from a Mr. James Browning. Mr. Browning lived near the Road Church and was always a good horseman and an honest man. He bought the first draft stallion into Stonington, a Percheron, about 1909 or 1910.

He also had trotting horses. Josie was of that breed, a trotter. She wasn't fast but she was stylish. Mr. Browning used to go to New York City in the spring and buy a carload of horses which he turned out to pasture all summer. They were tired, worn out, sore-footed and lame from being driven on the city's hard pavement. The livery stables and cab horses had to go all the time. Their owners could not afford to rest them very long or they would lose money. They could keep just so many, so each horse had to work regularly.

Mr. Browning took a veterinarian with him and they would make a trip around the stables. Dr. Critcherson, the vet, would examine the horses and those which weren't hurt seriously, they would buy. And buy them cheaply. When Browning had enough for a carload, he would bring them to Stonington and turn them out on the farm for the summer. They would heal rapidly on good grass and water and rest all summer. When fall came they would be sound and could be sold back to the city at a good profit to go to work again.

When I traded for Josie, Mr. Browning was an old man. He had a brother to Josie which would kick a buggy or a wagon all to pieces quick. He was turned out to pasture and was considered worthless because he couldn't be driven. I asked

Mr. Browning if I could try to break him and he said yes and he would pay me if I could.

I saw a chance to have some fun and maybe make a little money at the same time. I charged $25 to $35 to break a colt and I handled six or seven and they were going fine. Their owners were very pleased with them. I first broke two for Herbert West, then two for Richard Wheeler, one for his father, Silas Wheeler, one for Sandford Billings and one for Thomas Wilcox. These colts were nearly all sired by Mr. Browning's stallion.

I went with Mr. Browning to the pasture to get the kicker. He carried some grain in a pail and the horse came right up to him. He was gentle in all ways but was afraid of a wagon. He wouldn't run, just stand and kick it to pieces. We put a halter and war bridle on him and I led him home, riding Josie. We had no trouble at all.

The next day I took him out and threw him on his side. He had had so much of this that he simply lay down for me. Throwing a horse is the first part of its subjection. Someone had tried to break him and had used this method until he wouldn't fight anymore. My breaking harness had two small rings each side of the crupper. They were put there for a purpose. I took two one-gallon oil cans, punched a hole through them and hung them on a piece of window sash cord about four inches apart to which I attached a snap. I made two sets. Then I put on my breaking harness and rigged up the safety rope or running W.

I started him up. We went for a short distance then I tightened the rope and threw him on his knees. This was something new to him and he fought it hard. When he gave up to it, we hung tin cans on the crupper. Then we couldn't get near enough to him for two hours to take them off. He kicked all the time, kicked even while on his knees. Finally, he became so tired we could get the cans off, which we did and put him in the barn. He wasn't subdued, just tired out.

The next day we did it all over again but he quit his kicking sooner. We kept this up about a week. then hitched him to a rig. It was a pair of front wheels and I drove him.walking behind it. I had on a hitching strap which went over the horse's rump and is fastened to each shaft. When he kicks, the strap holds him down. This is prevention, not cure.

We had gone nearly three miles without the cans and things were going fine. I thought I would test him a little so I pushed the butt of the whip up under the harness over his rump. Before I could tighten the safety rope he kicked and broke a shaft. I didn't test him anymore and we came home all right. But I had found out something. He had an area on his left rump where the muscles were hard and tight, not soft and relaxed as they should be. It was about the size of a teacup saucer. When anything touched it, he would tighten up and kick. He was perfectly gentle every other way.

Apparently, he had been injured there in some way sometime and he was afraid he was going to be injured again. My job now was to convince him that he wouldn't be hurt when touched on that spot. I took a long pole or one long enough so he couldn't reach me and wrapped a soft bag around one end. I asked my friend, John Schiller, to help me. We put on the war bridle which he worked while I touched the spot with the pole.

It was funny, he was soft and relaxed all over his hind quarters except at that one place. I began lightly touching the area. If he tightened up or began to John would jerk the bridle and punish him some. Not too hard, just enough to stop him. After one half hour or so, you could touch him rather roughly with the bag and he didn't mind. I knew we were coming with him. We kept this up for several lessons then hitched him up again. I tested him carefully with the whip again and he was all right. I drove this horse all around the town with the tin cans on his rump every day for three weeks. No trouble. I had a two-wheel cart I used for breaking. One day I drove him over to Mr. Courtland York's farm and Mrs. York took a picture of the horse cart and tin cans.

I took the horse back to Mr. Browning, told him what I had done and he was very pleased about it. I advised him to always use a kicking strap, just in case. He turned the horse out to pasture, then kept him in the barn for winter.

On Christmas Day he hitched this horse to a buggy and drove him four or five miles to a neighbor's house, Amos Wheeler's, where he had been invited for Christmas dinner. He unhitched, put the horse in the barn for the day, then hitched him again and drove home without the least bit of trouble.

I saw Mr. Browning the next spring, when he told me about it. He said they were so surprised to see him driving this kicker. But he had bad news. He had lost the horse during the winter with colic. He gave me a nice purebred Berkshire sow pig and fifty fawn-and-white Indian Runner duck eggs for breaking the horse. I set the eggs and they hatched well. We raised a lot of ducks and I kept them for years. One year, I had about seventy.

I remember one time a friend of mine, Cliff Stimson by name, bought a horse from one of his neighbors. I don't recall the neighbor's name but it might have been Bill. Anyway, the horse was a very good one, sound and well-mannered and gentle. Cliff wanted this horse and had been trying to purchase him previously but Bill wouldn't sell. Hearing that Bill wanted to raise some money and would probably sell the horse to get it, Cliff went over to see him. Yes, he would sell the horse and price was $200.

Now, Cliff wanted that horse very much and his neighbor knew it. He made up his mind to hold out for all he could get because Cliff wanted it so badly. On the other hand, Cliff knew his friend was short of money and practically had to sell the horse to get it. Still, Cliff was pretty careful with his money and didn't intend to fool any of it away. Cliff said he would rather pay $100 for the horse than $200. Bill said that most everybody would. They kept this up until they got the price to $150.

They stuck there. Neither would give an inch. Each knew the other had had his last say. "If you want this horse, Cliff," said Bill, "You bring the money over and come get him in the morning." "Look, Bill," said Cliff, "I will buy the horse if you will shoe him for me and I will take him tomorrow morning. Now that isn't much just to shoe him, is it?"

Bill thought for a moment and then said it would cost him $5. He repeated that it would cost him $5 but said he would do it. "All right," said Cliff, "I will take the horse." He pulled out a roll of bills and walked over to his friend and began counting out the money. When he came to $145, he stopped. "Since you are willing to spend $5 to get him shod, I don't want him shod anyway. We will take the shoeing off the $150 and I will be over to get him in the morning." And that was the way Cliff bought the horse.

I used to know two men who were managers of Guernsey cattle farms, Guy Williams and Ted Browning. I would purchase purebred bull calves from them to use in my herd to improve my stock.

I would raise the heifer calves for replacements in my herd and would have good young stock. No farmer could afford to sell his best cows. Therefore, you had to raise them yourself. To keep a milking herd at top level, you should raise one heifer calf for every three cows you have each year. This will just about make up your losses caused by accident and disease. When a cow injures her udder so she doesn't milk from all four quarters, we turn her out to good pasture for summer to fatten her cheaply on grass. Then we butcher her for home use in early winter.

The price I paid Guy and Ted for these bull calves was $25. No price at all for purebred bulls with their registration papers furnished. You know, Ted told me, we get $1,000 for this bull if you do not want him. I asked him how come he would sell him to me for $25. "Well." said Ted, "It is this way. We will take him to a Guernsey cattle auction and find a friend there who has a bull calf to sell. We each agree to buy each other's calf and pay $1,000 for him. That sounds big when the prices received at the sale are announced. makes people think Guernsey cattle are in great demand and expensive. Actually.

all we do is trade calves but they are sold for $1,000 each." Big deal.

One day I was visiting Guy and saw a beautiful Guernsey cow in a box stall. She had just had a fine bull calf and Guy said she was sold for $600 to go to California. But not the calf. They didn't want that but I sure did. Guy was very reluctant to let me have it but wouldn't tell me why. It wasn't the price, which was $25, but some other reason.

Finally he consented to let me have the calf but on one condition. I was not to use him except on the first cross. I could keep his heifer calves but they would have to be bred to an unrelated bull. I agreed and so got the calf. He was a beauty and I bred him with all my cows. When his heifer calves freshened. they, as a group, gave more milk than any I ever had before. So much so, that I decided to go one more cross. I told Guy about it and again he strenuously objected to the second cross. But I went ahead and did it anyway.

Then I got into trouble. I found out why Guy didn't want the second cross. This family of cows had a serious inherited fault. As they went into the eighth month of pregnancy, the cervix would swell and enlarge to the point where it would protrude from the vagina as large as a football. Then we would have to push it back in. The next time the cow would lie down, out it would come again.

After she calved, in two or three days, it would shrink back to normal size and she would be all right again. Guy knew this and although this family gave lots of milk they all had this fault. I had to get rid of all of the second cross. I later asked Guy why he sold the dam of the bull I bought from him to California and he laughed and said that that was as far away as he could get her.

Now, one day Whit and I were working in the tool shed. A cattle truck drove into the yard with a nice looking horse in it. The man said he heard I wanted a horse to work and thought I might like this one.

The man's name was Angelo. I did want another horse just then as my colts weren't old enough to do heavy work.

Angelo said this was a colt and wanted just a little breaking which he was sure I could give it.

Now, I knew Angelo. He was a sharp trader and couldn't relax and sleep peacefully nights unless he cheated two or three different people that day outrageously. I knew I would have to be on my guard and not relax for a moment. The horse looked like she could do a lot of work and I wanted her. I also knew she must be some outlaw horse Angelo had picked up somewhere and thought to stick me with. I had no doubt that I could make her work but it would require some time to train her.

She had shoes on her front feet which meant she had been worked at some time or other. I figured she probably was one which had gotten the best of her drivers and so had become an outlaw.

How old is your colt, I asked Angelo. I guess about four or five, he said. I looked at her teeth and they indicated she was eight years old.

"She is eight, Angelo," I said. "Well, you know how time flies," he replied. "It seems only yesterday she was a colt and we still think of her as being a colt."

"Yes, I know," I said. "How much do you want for her?"

"Well, I will have to get $65 for her and she is worth much more. I think you won't have much trouble with her, just a little breaking is all she needs," Angelo replied.

Sixty-five dollars, that wasn't much. Now I knew she was an outlaw because he wished to get rid of her so badly. But I also had something which I wanted to get rid of just as badly. It was the last of those cervix cows and she was almost ready to calve. I had been pushing that thing back three times a day for a month.

"Sixty-five dollars, Angelo?" I said. "How about $50? I haven't got that much money in cash just now but if you could wait a month I will have it then. Fifty dollars is enough for this horse anyway."

"No," he shook his head. "I want $65 but if you haven't got the cash maybe you have something you would like to trade, a cow or calf or something."

I had a cow and she was something all right, no question about that. "Well," I said slowly, "I do want this horse and I do have a cow I might trade if you will give me enough for her as she is worth much more than the horse."

I caught Whit's eye and jerked my head towards the barn. He left us talking and disappeared. After a few minutes, I took Angelo to the barn to see the cow Whit was working around. The cow was standing up and everything was all right. Angelo looked her over, bumped a calf in her side and asked the price. I said $75. He finally agreed to take the cow in exchange for the horse and the trade was made. I put the "colt" in the barn. He loaded the cow in his truck and drove off.

The next day before I left to go on the milk route, I told Whit to get the "colt" out and hitch her up. I felt sure he would have a time doing it but Whit is a very good horseman and I knew he could do it, and he did. He used the war bridle and running W, both. He threw the "colt" just one hundred and one times before she would stand to be hitched.

She was just what I thought she was, an outlaw who had gotten the best of her former drivers. She had worked enough to know how to work but she just wouldn't do it. This time she had to do it. That afternoon we hitched her up to a mowing machine and mowed with her. We kept the running W on her for two or three weeks. Then we took it off as she didn't need it anymore.

One day before we removed it we had a visitor to the mowing field. He stood with a couple of other fellows at the edge of the field watching Whit mow. When Whit came around to where they were standing, it turned out to be Angelo and two of his pals. They looked bug-eyed at the running W, having never seen one before, and were they surprised to see the "colt" working so quietly and willingly.

Angelo never did get over it and, when at the different fairs he would see Whit, he would call out loudly and proclaim to the crowd, "That boy can drive anything with hair." He seemed very proud to have us as his friends. I took the "colt" business as a joke as he did the cow. He sold the cow to one of his pals and got a good cussing-out when they discovered about the cervix.

John Lawrence and Sally Davis's five-year-old son, Whit, John Whitman Davis, in 1929, pulling reins in the farmyard. He grew to be an expert horseman.

Whit shared his father's love for horses. Above, Whit, about 16, with his new colt, Blaze, and, below, a few years later. An image of Blaze has been carved on Whit's gravestone.

CHAPTER 15

HAYING

When the barns are all full of hay that which is left over is stacked. A stack is a pile of hay or corn fodder so heaped that it will shed water. It will be used by moving it into the barn when the barn becomes empty enough to hold it or fed out-of-doors to the stock once a day until the stack is used up.

If some hay gets wet, and some always does, we stack that and feed it outside. Hay which becomes wet after it has been about half cured never dries out thoroughly and if put in the barn or baled it gets musty or moldy because it cannot get air through it to dry it out. A stack is out in the wind and air and can dry better. It keeps quite well. Of course, good dry hay can be stacked also, and is, when there isn't room in the barn.

Now there are two different types or shapes of haystacks. One is the round type which goes up to a point at the top. The other is the oblong stack which is built with straight sides and ends and is topped off with a peak like the roof of a house. This shaped stack we use for bedding hay (salt marsh) because you begin at one end and going in about three feet come straight down from the top to the ground. This doesn't disturb the rest of the stack and insures you a supply of dry hay until the stack is all gone. There is no limit to the length of this type of haystack and you can use from it all winter long by just working in from one end. Of course, marsh hay is much shorter than upland hay so it comes out of the stack more easily.

The oxen Duke and Tige, heavily loaded with hay in 1916.

In stacking hay we only use a wagon or truck when we wish to haul it where it will be fed out through the winter. This is near the barn by the back of a wall or a fence so it can be fed over the wall to the stock without their being able to get to the stack itself as this would tear it to pieces and waste most of it. We spread it on the ground in small heaps, about what the stock will clean up in four or five hours of feeding.

The stock is put back in the barn and fed again for the night. By feeding out, it saves a feeding from the barn where the hay is already stored, gives the stock exercise all day and all the water they want. On stormy days, they are let out of the barn only to drink.

When spreading the hay or fodder in the feed lot I was told to be sure none stayed by the wall as the boss cow might push another cow against the wall with her horns and injure her. I am reminded of just such an accident which happened on a farm near here just a few years ago.

They had built a pole fence around the haystack to protect it from the cows. However, they had neglected to saw off the ends of some of the poles, which protruded five or six feet beyond the corner posts. Apparently a cow had been feeding near this end of the pole or rail and had been attacked by another cow which pushed her so hard against it that it entered her stomach to the depth of three feet or more. In her desperation to get away she broke off the end of the rail by the post. When found, she was walking around with it sticking out of her side two feet long. Of course she had to be butchered. It goes to show what might happen. You cannot be too careful.

In stacking hay which you intend to move into the barn (as in a big meadow) the best and quickest method to get it to the stack is to sweep it in. Sweeping is as old as the hills and is done in this way. It is so fast you can mow down a larger acreage than if you were putting it into the barn.

Rake the hay into large windrows, the larger the better. Then turn each windrow over into dry ground so there will be no dampness under the hay. We always use a team of horses hitched to a front gear. You could also use a tractor in place of the horses. Next, tie both ends of a long heavy rope to the front gear with the loop dragging twenty-five or thirty feet behind. Beginning on one end of the windrow, straddle the row with the team and drive ahead until the end of the loop touches the hay and then stop the team. A man then stands on the end of the loop to hold the rope down near the ground so it won't be drawn over the top of the hay.

Now drive the team ahead slowly and the hay will gather in the loop. It takes two men, one on each side, to hold the rope down. Stops must be made often to adjust the rope properly. The men or boys standing on the rope should stand with toes pointed in and heels out and be careful not to get their legs inside the rope or they will get them pinched.

I like to work with horses as there is no noise and they will stop when they hear the man on the rope call out "whoa" before the driver could stop them. I have seen this happen many times and, in sixty-five years of sweeping hay, I have never yet had anyone injured. But all hands must be constantly alert or something might happen.

The boy who boarded here, Burt Wagner, used to drive the team for sweeping. He was from the city but I showed him how to handle the lines and drive and he took to it like a duck takes to water. He handled the team of colts to perfection and never once fell off the front gear on which he was standing.

When the rake has gathered all the hay, the horses can easily pull it to the stack. One end of the rake is then untied from the gear and the team is driven straight ahead pulling the rope out from the load where it trails back of the gear. Then back for another load. The boys used to grab the end of the rope and be pulled along by the team, sometimes on their bellies, sometimes sitting down. We would take the end of the rope in one hand, run ahead till we got a little slack, then with an over-arm swing send a coil along the rope as big as a barrel hoop all the way to the front gear. What fun we had. No one thought of it as work.

There had to be two or more at the stack, one to pitch and one to place it around on the stack. To make the stack go up straight to shed water we would pull in the loads after we got it started, first on the north side, then the south side, then the east side, and then the west side. Pitching from one side only would make the stack lean as the stackmaker would unconsciously build the stack up from whichever side it was being pitched from.

Sweeploads pitch easily as the hay is packed so tightly it is almost like baled hay. Start from the back of the load, never from the front. You can't pull it out from in front but it comes away easily from the back. We can put up a four-ton stack in about three or four hours. Most stacks are from two to three tons. We used to have twelve to fifteen such stacks before we built the addition on the cowbarn which holds forty ton or loads. I estimate a load as a ton.

When I was a boy and up until 1924 or 1925, all hay, as well as all manure and wood, was hauled by a pair of oxen on a two-wheeled cart. These carts (we had two) were built to stand heavy loads. The tires were six inches wide and the wheels five feet high, making the body two and one half feet off the ground. They were tip carts and could straddle rocks and tree stumps with ease.

Tom Burrell, who worked here on the farm for fourteen years, was very much attached to the oxen although he didn't care for horses. He and the oxen got along fine together. I drove the horses. We would both go to plowing in the same field at the same time, two plows working nine hours a day each. We did the field (five acres) in three days. I remember my hands would get blistered from the plow handles and I would wrap my handkerchief around the handle grip to ease the sores.

But back to haying. After the hay had been mowed, cured and raked up into good-sized piles, Tom would load it on the ox wagons and I would make the load. As the carts were two-wheeled and would tip, I had to make a load that would balance perfectly. If too heavy in front, it would bear down on the oxen's necks and make it hard for them. If too heavy in the back, it would "hang up" and choke the oxen by bringing the bows up against their throats. I would keep rocking the load back and forth until I had it just right. When the cart was loaded we would bind the load with ropes and then bring it to the barns. The barns were built to drive the load in. The oxen were unyoked and led out between the load and the cow mangers, then yoked again and used to pull the hay fork up to the peak of the barn where it slid over to the hay mow on a track.

The tripline was then pulled and the forkful of hay was deposited in the mow. It was then spread around and tramped down. For years I used to mow it away all alone. Sometimes another fellow would help. That made it easier.

I remember one time Uncle hired a fellow to help out for a week or so. One day after the fellow left Uncle asked Tom how the fellow worked. He was big and rugged and looked as if he could stand a lot. Tom replied, "Yes, he could stand a lot all right. Every time I looked at him he was standing. He just didn't do anything." Then how Tom did laugh.

Tom and I used to have fun betting each other what time it was. The wager was five cents. Tom had a watch and every five minutes or so we would guess the time. The one who came the nearest of course won. Neither of us intended to pay the other but it was fun to see how much we owed. Surprisingly, we wouldn't be too far apart at the end of the day.

Tom left this neighborhood around 1923 or so and went to live with his family over on East Avenue in Westerly, Rhode Island. He got a job over there working in the cemetery. One day on my way home I stopped by to see him. I said I had a man helping me with the hay but he wasn't much good and I didn't know when I would finish. Tom thought a minute and then said, "Boy, I think I can get a week off and, if I can, you and I are going to do some haying if we can get the weather. I want 50 cents an hour." Knowing my man, I thankfully agreed. I was giving my man a home, and I mean giving, because he didn't earn it, $2.50 for eight hours.

The next day Tom said he could come and would be here Monday. Saturday night I laid off the other fellow. Tom came Sunday morning and we did most of the Plum Bush (a fifteen-acre field) in one week. Some of it was planted in corn. I paid Tom $24 and finished my haying. That was the first time I ever paid 50 cents an hour. It would have taken me a month with the other fellow.

Now hauling hay with oxen or horses and pitching it on the wagons by hand may seem a slow and laborious process but, when I think back and consider that we would start our haying on the Fourth of July and finish by August 10, it makes me wonder.

Today, we have too much machinery to depend on. It is always breaking down and then you have to wait for a part to come and then you have to fix it. That all takes valuable time. I am not against machinery; it is a great thing when it is working smoothly. But it is a pain in the neck when it isn't. Now I suppose I shouldn't find too much fault with machinery but I remember the collar sores the horses used to have and how we padded the collars to prevent them or to help heal them up.

When the teams were through for the day we would thoroughly wash all sweat and dirt from their necks and shoulders, leaving them clean and smooth to dry. We used cold water from the well for this purpose, as cold water seemed to toughen the skin. In the spring, we treated the necks of the oxen in the same way until they became sufficiently hardened not to need it. But the teams were always ready for work and the work got done. It wasn't expensive either. The last plowing was done in May and the oxen would be turned to pasture for the month of June for a good rest. They were not used for the cultivating of the crops of corn and potatoes. Haying would begin July 1 and then the oxen would be used again through the daytime but turned out again at night. The horses the same.

I will now say a word about the supposed hard work of pitching hay. You can make it hard work or you can make it easy work depending on how you do it. There is a right way and a wrong way. When I hire green hands to pitch hay I let them work a while any way they choose. They will push their pitchfork into a heap of hay, lift out some, and then put it on the wagon. They keep this up until the pile is finished. About the fifth or sixth heap I stop them.

"Now, boys," I say, "How many forkfuls of hay did you take out of that last heap?" The answer would be four or five. "Now," I tell them, "How would you like to put it all up here on the load in one forkful and not work any harder than you are doing now? As a matter of fact, it will be so easy you won't believe it."

"We can't lift that much at one time," they would say.

"All right, I will show you how to do it." I get off the load and quickly make the heap into one big pile. Then, on one side next to the wagon, I run my fork under one-third of the heap, lift it up a ways, carry it two-thirds across the heap and press it through the pile of hay right to the ground, Then I lift the hay enough to heel the end of my fork in the ground when I hold it with one hand and raise the hay on the fork with the other. The hay is then over my head on the fork like an umbrella. Reaching down toward the ground I raise the hay over my head to the height of the load, walk to the wagon with it and deposit it on top of load. It is done by balance after you raise it off the ground.

This is the correct way to pitch hay. It requires little effort and is fast. Then the boys would do it, each trying to outdo the other, making a game of it, seeing who could lift the biggest heap. Then I would have them pitch double, standing side by side. This was so easy sometimes they wouldn't even try to heel their forks, just lift it right up.

One fellow, Davis Malloy, who worked for me by the month for more than two years, was from the city, where he had been employed in a mill. I showed him about pitching hay and, after we had finished loading the wagon, I asked him how he liked it. He looked at me soberly for a minute and then said, "John, if anybody had told me I could lift that much hay at one time before you showed me that fork trick I would have considered them crazy." One day Dave was pitching to me and we were nearly loaded. The load was high and Dave was short, he couldn't quite get it on top. I shortened my grip on my fork and leaned down to help him. Just as he pushed up, I struck down and a tine of his fork stuck into the heel of my hand.

In no time my hand went numb and I couldn't move my three end fingers. This was 1923 and I was getting up at three o'clock in the morning, milking eighteen cows all alone and then milking them again at night. I couldn't close my hand, not to say anything about milking. I immediately went out looking for someone to help me milk. My friend, Harold Critcherson, who had a farm of his own to tend to, cows to milk, etc., came here at three o'clock in the morning and again at night and did my milking as well as his own.

When Ase or others would jab their fingers, they used to apply a cud of tobacco to the sore place and that was it. I chewed a cigarette to get it moist and bound it on my pitchfork wound. It worked so well I was back to milking again in about a week. When I told our family doctor, Dr. Hillard, about applying tobacco to my hand and how quickly and nicely it healed, he said, "John, I think it healed that way in spite of the tobacco, not because of it." Evidently, he didn't think much of the tobacco cure. But it worked as it always had, very favorably.

It took about twenty-five minutes to load a wagon with one pitching. A good big load, as high as a man could reach, with two men pitching, took about twenty minutes. We could also unload a load with the big hayfork in the barn in twenty minutes.

We always say:

Half your corn / And half your hay
Should be in the barn / On Candlemas Day [February 2].

Loading hay on a wagon in August 1928. John Lawrence Davis is on top of the pile, using a long pitchfork. Below, his son, Whit, sweeping hay in 1950 with Whit's son Carter.

CHAPTER 16

CORN

Another important crop on any livestock farm is corn. It has been said, and rightly so, that corn is king.

The fodder, stalks and leaves, is fed out in two ways.

Some is put up for silage and some is fed as dried stalks. I have used silos for years and they are all right but they are expensive to fill. Often, a great amount is lost through spoilage (moldy and rotten). It often freezes to the side of the silo and to me silos are very unsatisfactory. They are expensive to put up and maintain and are taxed for full value like your other farm buildings.

Most silage is now piled in great heaps and covered with plastic to keep out the air. It is dug out of the heap with a bucket loader and carried to the cows in a truck either in the barn or out in the feed lot where it is put in large troughs or feed bunks. This is on large dairy farms. One dairy farmer near here last year planted and harvested 154 acres of corn.

The first silo I had was purchased in 1920. It was made by Green Mountain Silo Company, Rutland, Vermont, and cost me $300. It cost about another $300.99 to set it up. It lasted until it rotted out. Then I pulled it down and also another one I had. Then I went back to the old way. Instead of silo corn I raised the New England johnnycake corn, which is a flint corn. The silo corn is a dent corn. The New England or Rhode Island johnnycake corn is far more nutritious than the dent. We put this corn fodder in shocks to dry and then husk it and store it in the corn crib. The stalks are then stacked and fed to the cows from the stacks. This eliminates costly equipment and the cost of silage. Cows do fine on the corn stalks and leave hardly any butts after feeding. If we don't have time to husk all we raise, we just feed it to the cows unhusked, ears and all. That gives them lots of good grain.

The corn in the crib is picked over and the best is sold to the grist mill for johnnycake meal. The last we sold gave us $3 per bushel on the cob, a good price. Very few farmers raise this kind of corn now as the dairy farms haven't time to bother with it. They want big crops of silage corn which they can chop up in a hurry and get through with the job.

About 1909 we got our first corn planter. It was an Eclipse and planted one row at a time, including both seed and phosphate.

Before we had the planter, we planted by hand. When the seed was ready to plant, the field was harrowed with a light plow. The rows were three feet apart. The hills were spaced three feet apart in the rows. To get them square a long pole was used, to which three light chains were attached, spaced three feet apart. This was carried across the furrowed rows and, where each chain mark crossed the rows, a hill of corn was planted. This made the rows of corn run both ways across the field and the corn could be cultivated both ways. This saved hoeing between the hills.

With the corn planter we couldn't space the rows both ways so we had to hoe the ground between the hills. This made hard hoeing. I overcame this by buying and using a weeder which is a light, long-toothed harrow. Weed seeds sprout and come up a few days before the corn. The idea is to stir the ground on top of the planted corn but not deep enough to disturb it. This destroys the weeds as they are sprouting but doesn't hurt the corn.

Before a new crop of weeds can start the corn is up and can then be cultivated. About the third or fourth day after planting the weeder should be put on and kept on until the first corn begins to show. When about four or five inches high the corn should be cultivated, going twice in a row and pushing the soil up close to the plant, completely covering the ground.

I used to grow fifteen or more acres of silo corn in this way, got good crops and never used a hoe. But let me stress this fact: You have got to get there on time with the weeder and cultivator or you will have the weeds too high to control.

We are afraid of pesticides, so we do not use them, although most farmers do. I tried some a few times, got another farmer to do the work with his equipment, but the results were not too satisfactory. I would rather have a weeder and cultivator.

I remember one time when we planted corn by hand. My father kept me out of school two days, a Thursday and a Friday, to help plant corn. Father would drop the phosphate, a tablespoon at each hill, and I would kick some soil over it so it wouldn't burn the seed and then drop four, five or six kernels of corn in each hill. This was 1906 or 1907. I worked that Thursday, Friday, and Saturday, but was sent back to school on Monday.

I liked it. I remember I would run ahead of the others and claim I was the first man in the field. We were taught to work in those days and to take pride in our work as well.

I am reminded of a man with a large family who lived here in the neighborhood. One of the growing boys hired himself out for a few days to a farmer to help with the hoeing. When the job was finished and he returned home his father asked him if he got paid and how much. The boy told him and his father looked at him a minute then smiled. He said, "Well, I guess my boy has grown to be a man." He had been paid a man's wages.

I went into the field with the grown men and hoed with them all day. Tom would lead, then would come my Uncle John, then Uncle Sam Tefft, and I would bring up the rear. I would try hard to keep up with the others. I would get behind twelve or fifteen hills, then come to four or five hills which had been hoed out beautifully. Uncle Sam would hoe his own row and still find time to help me out. What a kind old man he was. He showed me how to clean my corn hill with four strokes of hoes instead of the six or seven I had been doing. This did away with those extra strokes and helped me to keep up.

We would break the ears off the silo corn and leave them in rows across the field until the corn fodder had been all put in the silo. The stalks were cut and laid in piles on the ground, just what a man could pick up. These were loaded on a wagon and carted to the silage cutter and dumped. Two men worked there placing it on the cutter table where an endless chain carried it to the blades and fan which cut it into small pieces and blew it up the pipe and into the silo. A man inside would spread it around and tramp it down.

It took eleven men to make a full gang and two or three teams to haul. We used to fill my silo, which was twelve by twenty-eight feet, in one day and a half. The men received 50 cents per hour. There were about fourteen silos in the neighborhood to fill and we all went from one silo to another until the work was done. Later, I bought my own cutter, blower, and engine. I could fill then with a small gang but it took longer. However, I didn't have to pay $25 for the cutter and, with the engine, I could saw my own wood whenever I wanted.

The ears of corn back in the field were brought to the barn and we used it for "husking bees." Some would go for the pigs and geese unhusked. That which was husked was put into the crib and fed out later. One year we had 800 bushel. That was the most I ever raised, all of it silo corn.

Of course, I planted some johnnycake corn too. Pumpkins were planted among the corn. I liked to see the corn all shocked with yellow pumpkins around on the ground. One time, Bill Surber, a great friend of mine, and I were gathering pumpkins in the corn field. I was in the wagon and Bill would toss them to me to catch. Bill tossed some a little too hard and I began to throw some small ones back at him. I had a good supply in the wagon and drove him back of a corn shock. I saw which one he was hiding behind and I thought I would surprise him. I jumped off the wagon, picked up a big heavy pumpkin and going to his shock I tossed it through the corn tassels at the top of the shock. I then ran off some distance and turned to see how my strategy had made out.

Bill was lying flat on the ground. Thinking he was fooling, I approached him. Bill wasn't fooling. He was knocked out cold. I thought I had killed him. I had never seen anyone knocked out before and I was scared. I shook him and finally he came awake. It seems that just as I tossed the pumpkin, he parted the tassels to look through. The pumpkin hit him square in the face. He didn't know what hit him and I didn't know he was there. Boys will be boys.

Uncle Sam used to say to me, "Johnny, one boy, half a man. Two boys, no man at all." Then he would laugh. But we worked hard and we played hard and we made light of the work and enjoyed doing it.

It took about three weeks to fill my silo after I got my own engine and cutter. During that time I hired what extra help I could get besides the two boys who worked here by the month.

Clarence Bailey was one of my regular men and he loved to box. I had a set of gloves and noontimes he would hurry through his dinner and box with the boys. Each would try to knock each other's hat off. Clarence was good at it and how he would laugh at the others. It was all good-natured fun and there were never any fights or hard hitting.

One time, when the last armful of fodder went up the pipe which finished the job, the boys wanted to celebrate. They caught Jimmy Robinson, a young fellow who worked off and on for me for I guess ten years or more and was a mighty good fellow and great fun lover, took him down to the half barrel water tub in the barn yard, filled the tub with cold water from the well, took off his pants, and set him in the cold water, behind first. Jimmy flounced around and finally got out of the tub. Then he gave them a good cursing out and how they did laugh.

The johnnycake corn, or field corn as we always called it, would be ripe and ready to cut about September tenth to the fifteenth. Uncle always raised a small piece of rye every year, which was mowed carefully with a scythe and tied in bundles. We would beat the heads over the edge of a tub to get the seed for next year's planting. We used to sow it the last of October. Uncle always bound the shocks of corn with the rye straw. If the straw was brittle, he would soak it in the pond over night and then it wouldn't break when he twisted it around the corn. This was the way his father did when there wasn't any string to be had. Of course, later binder twine came into use and then we didn't bother with the rye any more.

After the corn was shocked, it was left to dry for ten days or two weeks before husking began. While the corn was drying we would used the time to dig the potato crop. Then Tom would take his whole family into the cornfield on Sundays. Weekdays, he and Kate, his wife, would husk. I think they got 10 cents per bushel in 1916. Before that it was 5 cents per bushel.

The bags of corn were emptied on the crib floor and then sorted and put in the different bins. The best ears were saved for seed to plant the next year. All the other good ears were for johnnycake meal and the small underdeveloped ears went for the geese and pigs to fatten them for fall and winter butchering. The fall of 1916 we husked and put in the crib 505 bushel of johnnycake corn.

I have a field corn which is colored blue and white. This is a true Indian corn and was raised by the Narragansetts down in Rhode Island. Wolcott Main told me that when a man named Randall came to Pawcatuck to farm about 1840, he wanted some corn to plant. So he went down to Rhode Island and brought home this corn. It gained favor with some of the local farmers and has been raised around here ever since. It is a tall, quick-maturing corn and is nice to hang on doors in October. The quality is good too. I guess I am the only one to plant this corn now as not much field corn is raised anymore, just silo corn.

I have long had the feeling that a great many farmers do not know what they are missing. All they know or care about is milk. They feel they have got to make a great quantity of milk no matter what the cost to produce it.

Unloading sacks of corn at the crib in 1916

Getting ready for winter: the farm's woodpile, 1927.

CHAPTER 17

WOOD

The farm woodlot is very important to any farm. From it you get timber and firewood if you manage it correctly. I was taught from early boyhood to be a conservator for my own good. I was taught to leave the trees for timber and to cut the "stag" trees for firewood. A timber tree goes high in the air with no branches except at the top. This makes for a good long log to take to the saw mill. The tree should be either white oak, which is the best, or red oak or maple or poplar or hickory.

Red oak doesn't last as well as one might expect but it usually grows straight and tall. It makes a very nice firewood, being straight-grained, and splits easily. It burns good and makes a hot fire.

White oak is a poor burning wood but a wonderful timber tree. The wood is hard and, if kept away from dampness, will last 300 years or more.

The house and barn here on the farm were built in 1680 and are framed with oak so hard that a nail can be driven into them only with greatest difficulty. The floors are also of oak and perfectly hard and sound.

Maple is very good wood for burning. The rock or sugar maple and the swamp maple are good for timber.

Poplar, or white wood, is a good timber tree. It grows tall and straight and lasts a long time.

Hickory is a very hard tough wood. It makes good lumber. Ash is a good lumber wood too.

Sassafras is good lumber and grows straight and very tall. It is used for boards and fence posts. On this farm we had no soft woods except red heart cedar. It makes long-lasting fence posts if seasoned before placing in the ground. In fact, all posts should be seasoned before setting. There is a red heart cedar post holding a heavy gate now on this farm that was old when I was a little boy, seventy-two years ago. It is just as solid as it ever was. Also, some white cedar posts on a fence that was put in sixty-five years ago. They are nearly gone but are still standing.

I was instructed to cut the "weed" trees for firewood. A weed tree, or stag, is one which has branches near the ground and a very short trunk. The limbs are large, the tree broad and spreading. It shades the ground so the trees which are timber type cannot grow or little seedlings either. However, such a tree has a great deal of firewood in it and should be used for that purpose. So, in its way, it is valuable too.

We had four wood stoves here in the house and they used about twenty cord of firewood a year. We have three airtight stoves which burn all night in cold weather. We use white oak for this purpose, as it burns slowly and lasts all night. For a hot quick fire we use maple or red oak. Of course, the wood is cut and seasoned for a year before we burn it. Green wood is wood with the sap in it. Green wood will give you respiratory trouble like a cold. The sap in such wood will creosote the stove pipes and chimney also.

I was also told that when you cut down a tree to try to have it fall away from young growth which it might smash down as it crashed to the ground. Also, if a tree starts to fall toward you because of an error in judgment or a change of wind, do not run away from the stump or you will be caught by the branches and probably killed. Just step around the stump to the other side. Then you will be out of the way.

When you are trimming a trunk of its branches with an ax, stand on one side of the trunk and cut the branches on the other side. This keeps the trunk between the ax and you, protecting you from the ax. Always cut towards the top of the tree from the butt. Remember that the dull ax is the most dangerous to use as it will slip down along the side of a tree or limb, whereas a sharp edge will bite into the wood and will not slip.

When I was seven years old I wanted to split wood at the woodpile with Ase, whose job it was to split the winter's wood for the kitchen stoves. Ase would work at it off and on all winter. When he wasn't splitting wood, he would chop the next winter's wood in the woods by the cord.

On a cold, windy day, in the woods is a good place to work as the trees shelter you from the wind and the sun shines down to warm you. Chopping also keeps you warm. So cold days Ase would chop in the woods and when it was not so cold he would split.

The wood was always sawed the right length to fit easily into stoves and left in big piles for him to work on. I wanted to split too, so Father found me a hatchet shaped like an ax, put in a handle, and I was proudly in business. I remember Mother objected, saying I was too young for an ax and would cut myself. Father said no, I was all right, Ase would look out for me. Better I learn under the eyes of an expert than to wait until later and try to learn it alone.

Of course I always wanted to do as Ase did so he had no trouble teaching me to be careful. Sassafras wood splits easily and is straight grained. Ase would pick out some of this wood and pile it up around a little chopping block which was just the right height for me to use. He taught me how to stick my ax in a piece of wood, raise it over my head and bring it down on the edge of the ax to split it. Also how to start my ax in a piece of wood by holding it with one hand and bringing the ax down with the other. As you bring the ax down, remove your hand from the piece you are holding. Never strike unless you remove your hand first.

"Now," he would say, "I will show you how to split it into match wood like this." And he would carefully rest the edge of his ax on a narrow, thin bit of wood and gently lift the piece of wood about four inches off the block and then thump it down the block again which would set the ax just where he wanted it. Then he would split the piece. "Real fine, see how old Burns (his middle name was Burnside) does it," he would say. "Now you do it just as old Burns did." I would and he would laugh and tell me not to forget and to always do it that way. I always have.

I am here reminded of an incident which happened in later years. There was a fellow who took milk of me, got behind with his bill and asked to work some of it out on the farm. The only work I had at that particular time was splitting wood. I took him to the woodpile, gave him the ax, and showed him how to use it. I cautioned him about keeping the wood which he split away from around the block by his feet and told him everything I knew about safety.

That afternoon, as he was bringing the ax down on a piece of wood he was holding, his foot slipped and he cut his forefinger nearly off. We took him to the doctor, who promptly finished the job. It cost him a finger and me $300, which was luckily covered by insurance I carried.

In 1916, World War I was on. Ships were in great demand. The ships were made of wood so timber was high. We had a large wood lot on which the trees were about ready for cutting. At a certain age, a tree is hard. Then it gets brittle and isn't any good for lumber. These trees were still good and hard, mostly white and red oak with some black birch and maple and chestnut.

A lumberman who ran a sawmill came down from Norwich to look at and buy the timber. He made Uncle an offer and, after some deliberation, Uncle let him have it. The price was $2,500. Uncle was to have the tops for cord wood. The man only wanted the trunks. I think his name was Brocket and he was a very good and honest man. Uncle talked with Mr. Brocket and they agreed that, so as not to skin the woodlot, any tree whose caliber six feet from the ground was one foot was to be left. This was done, and due to my uncle's foresight I have good timber to use all my life from our woodlot whenever I need it.

It is so nice to go over in the West Woods and see white oaks that will cut a log twenty-five to thirty feet and two feet or more at the butt. That is conservation as it has been practiced on this farm always.

Mr. Brocket brought in two men to saw down the trees and cut them up into logs to be hauled to the sawmill, which wwew to be brought in after the logs were all cut. These men boarded in the neighborhood while they were working on the trees and they were expert in every way as regards the sawing down of trees. I would go over in the woods where they were working and watch how they did it. They were nice fellows and showed me all of the tricks of the trade such as how a tree would be leaning one way and they would make it fall another.

For instance, suppose a tree is leaning towards the west. You want it to fall either north or south. Now, every tree has to be scathed first, that is, a cut is made on the side of the tree in the direction you wish it to fall. The cut may be from three to six inches deep. Then the wood above the saw cut is chopped out as far back as the saw went: This is so when the tree falls the trunk won't split and spoil the log.

This tree leaning west is to be fallen north. It is scathed on the north side. Then it is sawed on a level with the scath, neither above or below. This is done with every tree; but in this case, as the saw approaches the scath from the south, more wood is left on the east side of the tree than is left on the west. This wood binds the trunk to the stump and keeps the tree from going down west. As the tree begins to weaken, a wedge is pounded into the cut from the south. This jacks the tree over to the north. Keep wedging until the tree leans heavily to the north, then keep sawing and wedging until the tree falls. This method, if carried out properly, works like a charm. Sometimes the iron wedge wouldn't be thick enough to tip the tree so the men would make thicker ones of wood. The wooden wedges wouldn't last very long but, when the tree was nearly cut through, they answered the purpose.

Of course, each kind of tree has its own individually shaped leaf. You distinguish a tree by its bark and leaf.

The sassafras tree is unique. It has three differently shaped leaves on each tree. One is a regularly shaped leaf and the other two take the form of a mitten. There is the body for the fingers and one for the thumb. Now, believe it or not, the tree grows a mitten for each hand, a right and a left. This has always been of great interest to me and when I am out in the woods in the autumn before the leaves fall, I look for young sassafras trees and for the mittens on them. Sometimes I bring some home to show to people who might be visiting here.

I have set out several thousand of white pine and white spruce trees during the past fifteen years or so. We use the white spruce for Christmas trees and sell boughs from the white pine for decorations. White pine makes beautiful bouquets and, combined with boughs of white spruce, makes beautiful sprays.

I think the old American chestnut tree will someday come back and bear nuts again as it used to when I was a boy. I know of some here at the farm which are around twenty feet high and I hope will have nuts soon. I know of one such tree, not on this farm, which is bearing now and had a crop last fall, 1970.

Another nut tree, of which we have three, is black walnut. It is a very sweet, delicious, meaty nut but has a very hard shell. The best way to open a black walnut is in a vise. Squeeze it lengthways just enough to crack it and usually the meat will come out almost whole. This is a most valuable tree for lumber and should be grown among other trees so it will have to grow fairly straight to reach the sun. Otherwise, it has tendency to branch early and so not make a good trunk for timber.

There are two kinds of hickory. One is called "pig walnut" and the other, "shagback." The pig walnut has a smooth bark and the nut is very hard and small-meated. The shagback has a very rough, shaggy bark and the nut is sweet and thin-shelled. It is easy to crack open. All the hickory in this farm's immediate vicinity is of the pig type so I imported some of the shagback and have two living, about fifteen feet high. They grow plentiful in North Stonington, which is where I got them. I also brought in some sugar maples and set them out on the farm. One is here by the kitchen and the others are down to the Trapper's Cabin. Some are large enough to tap.

We have a great many elderberry bushes on the farm. The berries make delicious jelly and wine. The bushes are about six or eight feet tall and have a pithy center. This pith is pushed out of pieces of a stalk about six inches long, and the hollow tube thus made is used to tap the sugar maples. We never made maple syrup, as there were no sugar maples here, but I have heard my uncle tell about how other farmers used to come here for the bushes for that purpose. This was before tin became plentiful enough to make spouts.

I am reminded of the story of the sailor who was shipwrecked on a small island. The only thing which came ashore from the wreck was a barrel of vinegar. There was nothing edible on the island but he noticed some bushes which, upon examination, had a large, sweet-tasting, and nutritious pith. He lived on this and the vinegar for some six weeks, when the ship finally took him off. The captain of the rescue vessel wrote in the ship's log that the sailor seemed very active and full of pith and vinegar.

There used to be a man, John Seymour, in the neighborhood who was a sort of jack of all trades. He could do carpentering well enough to get by with and as there was always someone's house or other building to repair he was most always busy. He used to work here when there was repairing to be done and one day he asked my uncle if he could cut some firewood on the halves. "On the halves" meant that no money was exchanged for the wood or work for cutting it. He would make a number of piles, each the same size and when he finished the job the piles would be divided. He would take his half and Uncle would have the other half.

Wood is cut in four-foot lengths and packed in heaps four, six, or eight feet long. If it is a four-foot heap, which is half a cord, two stakes are driven into the ground four feet apart and braced on each end to hold them straight and firm. Then the four-foot wood is packed between them, making a pile four by four by four, a half cord. A six-foot-long pile is made the same way and is three-fourths of a cord. Of course, an eight-foot pile is a full cord. That is the way wood is measured and put up in the woods.

It is piece work and the chopper is paid by the cord. The price in 1916 was $2 per cord, up from $1.50 in 1912. I remember Tom would come for his money on Saturday night for the wood he had chopped during the week. When the weather had been bad, rain or snow, etc., which kept him from his work and Uncle would ask him how much he owed him, Tom would look down and kick the ground with his toe in an embarrassed manner. "I only cut four cord this week but I'd like to have ten dollars." Uncle would give it to him and Tom would pay it off later.

I used to go into the woods about one o'clock in the afternoon and come home at four o'clock. I cut and packed one half cord in three hours and I remember I sold six cord that winter to Hugh Schiller for $12 per cord in four-foot lengths and delivered. That was in 1943.

Whit would take a load of manure with the two-horse team, with a "spike horse" in front to help pull up the hill, making three horses, and bring back a half cord of wood. That made a load each way and we got along fine.

To get back to John Seymour. Seymour was closer than the next second about everything. When he wanted to cut wood at the halves, Uncle told him to go ahead and cut it and, when he was finished, they would divide it. In a week or so Seymour came to the house and said he was finished and was ready to divide the wood. Uncle went with him to the woods. Seymour had two one-cord piles and had done a good job. Now when you chop wood you of course make chips, which fly all around and are wasted. Seymour couldn't stand to lose those chips so, instead of using an ax, he sawed. That was all right and the wood looked fine. Beside each cord pile was a small pile of hoe-handle size poles which he had cut and racked very carefully. Uncle asked what the poles were for and Seymour said they were for firewood too, being the smallest branches. The wood was a good long mile from Seymour's house and as he had no horse or way of getting it home, Uncle asked him if he would like to have it carted. Seymour said no, he didn't want to pay for carting. He would get it home sometime, some way. Uncle said all right and left.

Seymour went home, got a wheelbarrow, and wheeled that cord of wood over a mile to his house. How many trips he had to make, nobody knows, but he got it all there finally. He then handsawed it into stove lengths with a bucksaw because he said a regular circular saw was thicker than his buck saw and would waste too much wood in sawdust. His nephew, Howard Brown, who lived just across the road from him would have been glad to saw it for him as he did custom sawing for a part of his living, but Seymour didn't want to waste the wood or pay anything for the sawing.

Seymour kept five or six hens to lay eggs for his own use. Since he had no cat or dog to feed, what they might have eaten in the form of table scraps went to feed the hens. In this way they could be fed very cheaply. If he had a few more eggs than he could use he would occasionally sell a dozen to some neighbor who might want them.

Howard also kept some hens, which he sold eggs from and I well remember the beautiful Rhode Island Red cockerels he would raise and fatten for the Christmas trade. He would have twenty-five or thirty and they would dress off at six pounds or better each. I used to do the same thing with chickens and still do with ducks and geese. The money comes in nicely for Christmas.

When Seymour's hens weren't laying he would buy some from Howard, for which he charged 25 cents a dozen. One time, Howard was short of eggs when his hens molted for about three weeks. Seymour's hens were laying and he sold Howard a dozen and charged him 30 cents for them. Seymour said the eggs were strictly fresh and therefore worth more than just fresh eggs. Howard said the eggs he sold were always fresh and, in telling me about it, he couldn't understand what

Seymour meant by "strictly." "A fresh egg is a fresh egg, isn't it?" he asked me. "One that has just been laid?"

"Yes it is," I said.

"Then," Howard replied, "What does he mean by strictly?"

"I guess it means in this case that he is getting five cents more a dozen from you than you charged him. That is the way it looks to me," I said.

Howard nodded his head in agreement and didn't buy any more eggs from Seymour.

One time, Uncle was in a store in town and there was fellow in the store who was telling the storekeeper how hard up he was, being out of work, and that he was looking for a job. He said he could do most any kind of work only he couldn't find any to do. The store owner asked Uncle if he didn't have some wood to be cut and could he give the fellow a job cutting it. The fellow was eager for the job and said he would ride back with Uncle and go right to work if Uncle would lend him an ax to work with until the next day when he would bring his own ax. Uncle brought him home, got an ax, and took him over to the woods and showed him where to chop. There was wood enough there to make five or six cords. The fellow took the ax and Uncle came home.

Late that afternoon the fellow came to the house, said he was coming along fine, had packed half a cord and had more lying on the ground which he hadn't packed. He said he was kind of tired and would Uncle take him the three miles back to town and lend him a dollar to buy himself a new ax the next day. He said he didn't mind walking down to the farm mornings but at night he was tired and would Uncle take him back to town at night.

Uncle felt sorry for such a worthwhile fellow and said he could be glad to do so. The request was not unusual; I remember a fellow named Hurt used to walk from Pierce Street to the farm to split wood in the winter and Uncle would carry him home at night and that was over four miles. Mr. Hurt had a dinner pail with a place in the bottom for coffee and, at a quarter to twelve, he would ask me to take it to the house and set it on the stove to warm the coffee. He was a very nice man.

Well, Uncle gave the fellow a dollar for his new ax and took him to town and left him. The next day the fellow didn't come to work, nor the next, nor the day after that. In fact he never did come back and Uncle never saw him again. But Uncle wasn't worried because he had a one half cord all packed up and more on the ground. The dollar he lent the fellow would just about pay for it so he wasn't out anything.

One day, Uncle had another fellow, Charles Thompson, come to the farm to chop wood so he thought he would take him to the place where the fellow who wanted the new ax had been working as that piece of wood was ready to be cut and Uncle wanted it cut. It was a small swamp area of maple wood and that fellow hadn't even stuck his ax into a single tree. He hadn't cut a chip, not one. Just stayed over there all day and then gotten a dollar out of Uncle at night.

Uncle was chagrined at being flim-flammed by a stranger he was trying to help but there was nothing he could do about it so he had to let it go. He vowed he would be careful about the next stranger who came around, he would be sure of that.

Mr. Charles Thompson was a cripple. He was married and had one child, Edith, who used to come to the Lower Pawcatuck School. Charles had hurt his back in some way which left him bent over forward so that, when he walked, his head was less than three feet from the ground.

He had a good garden during the summer and stored plenty of vegetables for winter use. He worked at whatever he could do all the time and his wife took in washing. This kept them going.

He wanted to chop wood and he put up two cord and two feet for Uncle, then became ill with a cold or grippe and had to stop working for the rest of the winter. He was a good, honest hard-working man. He used to buy johnnycake meal from us to be left at a neighbor's house near where he lived. Uncle would always put in a couple of pounds extra when he was weighing it up for him. He never knew about it.

There used to be quite a bit of boat building along the Pawcatuck River during the winter, skiffs and power boats which would be sold in the spring. For the bow piece, one piece of wood was desired. This made the bow strong and firm.

These pieces were called knees and were of white oak. When we found a tree with a very large branch extending straight out from the trunk we would carefully cut it down and saw off the limb four or five feet from the trunk making the "L." This would be put in a ditch where the salt tidewater could flow over it and it could be preserved in this way for years.

I remember four or five such knees in the ditch where I used to set my traps for muskrats. When the boat builders wanted one to use, they would come and get it out of the ditch and pay Uncle for it.

Horses and a wood sledge ready for the woods in 1934.

CHAPTER 18

DOGS

Every farm should have a good dog.

They protect the poultry and other livestock from dogs, foxes, raccoons, etc., and also the garden from woodchucks. Woodchucks do an awful lot of damage to a garden. Peas, cabbage, beans, pumpkins, and squash are all greatly relished by them and they will do an unbelievable amount of damage in just one night. If the garden isn't checked every day or so you may find one hundred feet of a row of these vegetables eaten right down to the gound. The greatest damage is done when the plants are four to six inches high.

A good dog that cruises around the farm hunting woodchucks is a very valuable animal, providing he stays home and doesn't run off with other dogs. If he does, he is a liability instead of an asset. Two or more dogs running together will kill poultry or sheep and, once they start on that, they can never be broken of the habit.

Dogs have an instinct to hunt and kill the right things instead of the wrong ones. We have dogs that are taught to hunt foxes and nothing else. These are fox hounds. Then there are coon hounds. They are taught never to follow fox, just raccoons. Then there are bird dogs. They are trained to hunt birds but if one of them gets out of hand and into a flock of poultry, the damage is apt to be great.

One such instance occurred near here. Two dogs broke into a laying house where there were about one thousand laying hens. The owner was away at the time. When he returned home, two and a half hours later, he found the dogs in the henhouse and 240 dead hens. The man to whom the dogs belonged had a real bill to pay.

When I was a boy, there were many dogs in the neighborhood. They were mostly collies and shepherds, not the German police dogs, and they were all good dogs, stayed home, minded their own business, drove cows to and from pasture, and hunted woodchucks.

Nearly every farm had a few sheep. The dogs, sheep, and poultry were all brought up together and everything went along very nicely. If a roaming dog from outside got into a flock of sheep, he was promptly shot by their owner, buried, and nothing was said. If the damage was much, the selectmen of the town were called in to appraise the damage, and the town paid the bill.

There was one farmer around, however, of whom most of us did not approve. He was a regular sharpie, owning land in two towns. One time, he had some sheep killed by dogs. He called in the selectmen from one town and they, after appraising the damage, paid him. He then immediately moved the dead sheep over the wall into the next town, called the selectmen from that town, and collected again. Sometime later, two of the selectmen from the two towns who were friends met and during the conversation mention was made of the sheep damage to the farmer. They compared notes; there was an investigation and a lawsuit. I have forgotten just how it did come out but it made quite a rumpus. Later on, this farmer was convicted of stealing cattle and served a term in jail.

Around 1904 or 1905, our farm dog died and Uncle bought a shepherd puppy. The pup was a pretty color, brown with a darker tinge to his hair. Uncle had little patience with training animals and while he liked the pup he considered him to be somewhat of a numbhead. (I am here reminded of the man who had a dog named Luke. Asked why he called him Luke, the man said he called him that because the dog wasn't so hot.) Uncle named the pup Joe Gump. He said Joe was the dog's Christian name but his surname was Gump. Gump stood for stupidity and good-far-nothingness and if ever a dog qualified along those lines, it was this one. He apparently didn't have a brain in his head and if he had any brains at all, they must have been in some other part of his body, the inference here being that they were located in that section of his anatomy most adjacent to his tail and Uncle said he didn't think he had any even there. They certainly weren't in his head, that was for sure.

Now Joe's first major experience with Uncle was when he developed the habit of sucking or eating eggs. He would get into the henhouse, get an egg out of the nest and proceed to eat it outside. Then he would go back and get another and so on until his appetite was satisfied. Uncle noted egg yolk on his muzzle one day and whipped him. That didn't do any good. It just made Joe afraid of him and he kept on eating eggs.

Uncle knew quite a few tricks and he made up his mind that he would teach that dog a lesson which he would remember. It would do him a lot of good, too. He got an egg, broke open one end and poured the contents into a teacup. He then added one teaspoonful of red pepper and mixed it thoroughly with the yolk and white. This he poured back into the shell. He carried this carefully out to the dog and set it on the ground nearby without spilling any of it. It was a full dose. Joe saw the egg, grabbed it, and began to chew. He quickly spat it out and held his mouth open for air. He smelled what was on the ground and then began to sneeze. How he did sneeze! Uncle said he thought the dog would sneeze his head off and if it hadn't stopped just in time he guessed he would have.

Joe lived to be over fifteen years old but he never touched another egg in his life. He was cured. This is an old remedy for egg-eating dogs and of the few cases I have known all were cured by this method.

Joe developed a habit for chasing hens. We kept around two hundred layers which had the run of the whole farm. The dooryard was full of hens all the time. Joe loved to run with all the speed he could muster and hit the hen, knocking her sprawling along the ground for a distance of ten or fifteen feet. He would then grab a mouthful of feathers from the back. These would fly up in the air in a cloud and what with the loud squawking of the hen, there would be quite a commotion.

This pleased Joe but he would look fearfully around to see if Uncle had witnessed his playfulness. He usually had, and Joe well knew what was coming next and he didn't have long to wait either. What came was whatever Uncle could find quickly to throw at the time — a stone, club, or the broom. These articles were used to emphasize the stern command to Get Out.

Joe would run for the cellar door and quickly disappear. Uncle, being lame, would not pursue him down there and Joe knew he would be all right. There he would stay until he deemed it safe to return from his hiding place. This went on two or three times a week throughout Joe's life and the dog never was hit once that I ever knew of. His ability to successfully dodge anything that was thrown at him from either a short or a long distance was positively uncanny.

Uncle would try hard to hit him a near miss. If the club was aimed in front of him, hoping he would run into it, Joe would slacken speed and the missile would pass in front of him. If coming straight for him, he would increase his speed and the rock would pass to his rear.

This frustrated Uncle no end. Why he couldn't hit that dog, he didn't know. When he went to school and they played Duck on the Rock, Uncle was champion. He could hit the duck almost every time from any reasonable distance but he couldn't seem to connect anything with Joe. But he kept trying, hoping that someday the dog would make a mistake and get hit. But he never did. He always dodged successfully.

Now Uncle didn't dislike Joe, he was only trying to stop him from chasing the hens. Otherwise, they got along pretty well. In fact, Uncle was rather proud because Joe was such a fighter. Whenever any of us went to town with the horse and buggy or wagon, Joe went also. He would trot along by the horse and, when reaching town, would lie by the wagon until we were ready to come home. Then he would come home also, trotting by the wagon as usual. Occasionally, he would be challenged by other dogs and then there would be a fight. These fights were very short and Joe always won.

One day, Uncle came home from town and was loud in his praise of Joe. It seems that two dogs pitched onto Joe at the same time, one small dog and one big dog. Joe grabbed the little one, shook him like he would a woodchuck, dropped him on the ground and then met the charge of the big dog shoulder to shoulder. Uncle jumped out of the wagon with the horsewhip in his hand ready to strike the other dogs and protect Joe. But Joe didn't need any help. He sent both of his assailants yelping up the street, pursuing them for a short distance and biting their flanks savagely to encourage them to greater speed. Uncle climbed back into the wagon, spoke to the horse, and continued on to town, Joe trotting along beside just as if nothing had happened.

We used to buy milk from some of the neighbors when we would be short in the summer. They would bring their night's milking to us in the evening. Uncle would empty their cans into his own and put them in the wooden tank which was kept full of ice water for that purpose.

One evening, a man named Fred came with his milk and had his big collie dog riding in the express wagon with him. Uncle came out of the house to take the milk and, seeing the dog on the wagon seat, told Fred he had better keep his dog in the wagon as Joe was around. There might be a fight and he didn't want Fred's dog to get hurt. Fred laughed and said he guessed his dog could take care of himself all right. He wasn't worried, so they went on into the milk room.

Joe walked over to the wagon, sniffed and whined a couple of times, then lifted one hind leg and soaked one of the wheels halfway up to the hub. This was more than the collie could stand. He jumped out of the wagon and pitched on to Joe. Such snarling and growling you never heard. The collie was a fighter all right and thought he would have everything his own way. Joe grabbed him by one front leg, twisted his head around and threw the collie on his back. Then Joe seized him by the throat and went to chewing there. Uncle and Fred came running out of the milk room, Uncle with the ever-ready broom, and they beat Joe off. The collie then limped to the wagon on three legs and finally managed to get in and back on the seat where he held up one paw and kept whining.

Fred was amazed. He said his dog had never been beaten before and wanted to know what kind of a dog Uncle had that could fight like that. Uncle said he was just a farm dog, nothing special, just a dog. But there was a twinkle in Uncle's eye when he said it. The next evening when Fred came with the milk, there was no dog with him. He told Uncle that Joe had broken the big collie's leg. The leg finally got better but it was weeks before he could put it on the ground.

We always kept sheep and Uncle was an expert at shearing. One hot summer day Joe came around panting with the heat. Uncle saw him and noticed how hot he appeared to be. "I will cool you off," Uncle said and then, to me, "Get the sheep shears from the shed." I got the shears and Uncle told Joe he was going to make him look like a lion. This he proceeded to do. He sheared Joe from his tail, on the end of which he left a tuft of hair, right up to his shoulders. When he got through, the dog looked like a black-maned lion. Heavy mane and tuft on his tail. Uncle was very pleased with the appearance of Joe but Joe wasn't so sure he liked it because, while he was cooler, the flies could now get to his skin and bite him. The hair soon grew out again and then he was his old self once more.

When Joe passed away, I got a Border collie pup and raised him up to be a good cow dog. He would drive cows beautifully but he was not a woodchuck dog. When he was about three years old, he disappeared one night. I think someone stole him as he was a very friendly dog as well as a pretty one.

Around 1932 or 1933, my wife's sister had a two-year-old dog which she had bought for a watch dog, but the only thing he watched was for something to eat. And that he never missed. I had seen this dog and thought what a fine farm dog he would make. So, when she asked me if I knew where she could find a good home for him, that she would give him away, I jumped at the chance and brought him home. He was a big old-fashioned kind of dog with a short muzzle. When I took him out to the barn he promptly killed one of my cats and went looking for more. That was a sign that he was a real hunter. He would make a good woodchuck dog.

I tied him up away from the cats and taught him to lie down at command. This took about three or four days, half an hour a lesson. I then got another cat; we had three or four more around the barn all the time to take care of the rats and mice which might come around. These cats were known as barn cats and were never allowed in the house. They were fed only milk in the barn and, if they wanted meat they had to hunt for it. And they did. I carried the cat in my arms to Andy — I named the new dog Andy — and made him lie down.

I approached him slowly with the cat. When he showed signs of attacking the cat, I would cuff him lightly with my hand saying, No, No. Then I would stroke his head and speak kindly to him and bring the cat closer. Soon he got the idea that I liked both of them. I let the cat go but kept him lying down. I brought the cat back to him and let him smell of it, all the time talking kindly to him and the cat too. Then I let him walk around the cat and soon he was perfectly indifferent to it. That job was done.

Now I had to teach him what to kill. I caught a woodchuck in a steel trap. I had knocked him half unconscious with a big stick and sicced the dog on him. Remembering the cat, he at first refused to cooperate. But I pounded the ground around the chuck and made all kinds of excitement like I was angry at it. He became excited too and grabbed the woodchuck which he shook till he killed it. I patted him, praised him, and showed him I was pleased about what he done.

He was a very intelligent dog and soon learned to hunt for woodchucks in the fields and wood. He would never touch a cat and I have seen cats curl up beside him and they would sleep together.

Andy would find a woodchuck out in the open meadow. He would circle around the chuck about six feet away, backing all the time. As he would circle, the woodchuck would keep following him around, always with his head toward the dog, ready to bite if the dog should attack. Soon, the chuck would tire of turning his head toward the dog and would stand and let the dog keep circling, only following around the circle with his head.

When Andy reached that part of the circle directly in back of the woodchuck, the woodchuck would be watching from the left side, then he would turn just his head toward the right to observe the dog from that angle as he came around the circle. That was what Andy had been waiting for. In just the short space of time while the woodchuck was turning his head and couldn't see, Andy would jump in, grab the chuck by the back, and shake him till he was dead.

Andy always hunted from down wind so he could scent the woodchucks but they couldn't smell him. In tall grass, he would jump up in the air trying to catch their scent above the grass. It was an education just to watch him. When he made a kill, he would bring the woodchuck to the house and show it to me. I would pat him and praise him, and how he liked it. Sometimes he would eat them, other times bury them to dig up later, but most of them I had to throw away.

In this manner I could count his kills. During the summer of 1935, he brought home or brought to me, 118 woodchucks. What a wonderful dog he was. He lived to become partly deaf and blind and one evening a car hit him in the head and killed him. He was the best dog I ever owned.

During the early 1920s, I bought a supposedly purebred collie pup for which I paid the then good price of $10. For this dog, it was $9.90 too much. He grew to be a thin-bodied, long-nosed, not-too-large a dog with a querulous disposition, always barking at nothing important and never paying the least bit of attention to something that was. He wouldn't look at a woodchuck, rat, or squirrel but would bark at every car that came around, including my own.

He would run along close to the front wheel and keep barking all the way from the house to the garage, a distance of two hundred feet or so. I tried to break him of this. I would stop the car, get out, and chase him away. When I returned to the car and got in, he was right back there again barking as before. I got tired of this. It was annoying and I decided to really do something about it. So I did.

The next day I started up the Model T Ford truck I had and headed for the garage. He was right on deck, barking at the front wheel. Now, in going to the garage, I always went in a straight line. The dog knew this and judged the distance from the front wheel accordingly. This time I opened up the gas full speed and pulled way over to the right. He was just in front of the right wheel. Before he knew what it was all about, I had run completely over him with the front wheel and, before he could get up, I ran over him with the hind wheel also.

I went into the garage like a whirlwind, succeeded in stopping before I went through the back end, got out, and went back to pick up my dead dog. Only he wasn't dead. He had managed to get up and was high-tailing it for the cellar, where he stayed for three days. The afternoon of the third day he was right back on the old stand, barking excitedly at the front wheel again. I gave up.

Don — that was the dog's name — was missing for two days one time. A neighbor living nearly four miles away telephoned me that a thin-looking collie had come to his place and was making himself right at home. He thought the dog belonged to me and, of course, it was Don. I brought him home, tied him up for a couple of weeks, then let him go. He did go, right back over to the four-miles-away farm. I brought him home, tied him up again and pondered what to do.

Finally, I decided. I had a fellow working for me who would do just as he was told, providing he felt like doing it. I told him what I had in mind and he said okay. He tied a string around Don's neck, took him over in the woods about a half mile from the house, fastened him to a tree with the string. With a twelve-gauge shotgun, he blew his head off. Of course,

Don wasn't seen around the house any more. My good Aunt Sarah missed feeding Don and inquired if anyone knew of his whereabouts. Nobody did. We hadn't seen him. He must have gone away somewhere but nobody knew where. She asked the hired man, whose name was Bill, and who had been warned not to tell, if he had seen Don. Bill said the last time he saw the dog, he was tied to a tree over in the woods.

My aunt turned up her nose, sniffed disdainfully and said, "How ridiculous, the idea, tied to a tree. I guess so."

But Don never came back and, as far as I know, he is still tied there.

CHAPTER 19

CATS

Back in the old days, a barn cat had a litter of kittens. A barn cat is one that isn't allowed in the house. It stays around the barn and is fed milk at each milking. If it wants meat, it has to hunt for it. That way, the number of rats and mice is kept down. That is the way it should be.

We always kept a few barn cats which were more or less wild and untamed, and they certainly could hunt. If any of them got to stealing young chickens, they would be shot. There were usually a few that wouldn't steal so they were good to have around.

Well, in this litter was a pure white kitten. It was so pretty that Uncle John took a fancy to it right away. He brought it in the house where he could feed it and pet it whenever he pleased. This was to be his house cat. This cat would like to climb up on Uncle John's shoulder and lie across his neck. He did this while Uncle was eating his supper. Uncle would put scraps of food in his dish on the floor and the cat would climb down and eat it.

Uncle named the cat Robert Henry. Robert Henry would perch on Uncle's shoulder and ride around the farm with him while he was doing his chores. They were great friends. Robert grew big and fat and Uncle was pleased and proud of him. Uncle would go to the kitchen door and call to the cat and, if it was nearby and could hear, would come right away.

Robert Henry was getting bigger every day and one fine day he presented Uncle John with a litter of kittens. Uncle was surprised and dumbfounded. "By Gosh," said Uncle, "I thought I had that cat figured right but we all make mistakes, I suppose I missed that one." After that, Uncle had to rename Robert Henry. He retained the cat's surname of Henry but changed its Christian name to Roberta, now becoming Roberta Henry. Roberta had her kittens in a big wooden box in the kitchen by the wood stove. I don't remember whatever became of those kittens.

Quite some time later, Uncle was sitting on a large stone by the toolshed when Roberta wandered by rubbing up against Uncle's leg. As Uncle reached down to pet Roberta, she grabbed him by the thumb, leaving quite a gash. I don't know what came over that cat to do such a thing to Uncle but he jumped right up and shook the cat off. I remember how his thumb did bleed from the bite. Uncle began looking around as he lost something so I asked him what he was looking for. He said, "I am looking for a club to kill that d____ cat with." Thus ended what had been a true friendship between animal and man.

Now, most farm families have a box or chest where all kinds of cure-alls are kept. Uncle had one and so did my father. These boxes contained camphor, Perry Davis pain killers, iodine, vaseline, liniment, clean strips of cloth, string, court plaster, skunk oil, castor oil, arnica and what we used to call "puffball." A puffball was a fungus that, when squeezed, gave off a dust. It was good to stop things that were bleeding. You would apply a puffball to a cut, then wrap it with strips of cloth. It always worked very well. I can remember going out into the pasture with my aunt and gathering the puffballs.

Another remedy was "pepper elixir." This was made by soaking the seeds of a hot pepper in vinegar. Father called it pepper sauce. The sauce was good for putting on beans or meat as a hot seasoning. We used to mix the pepper sauce with molasses for a sore throat. This remedy was approved by a doctor in Westerly who was an ear, nose, and throat doctor. The sauce was said to shrink the swollen tissue.

Now, Uncle needed something for his cat bite so he went to his medicine chest to get some pepper elixir. He used a goose feather to apply the elixir to the wound. It was pretty hot stuff, and Uncle never flinched from the smarting. After the bleeding stopped, he would stick his thumb in a jar in the elixir and just let it soak.

He didn't find a club while he was in the mood to use it so the cat got away. The cat never came in the house again after that. If it came near the door, Uncle would splash it with water, wetting it thoroughly.

Roberta soon got the idea she wasn't wanted around the house so she went to the barn with the other cats.

CHAPTER 20

COON HUNTING

I remember when we — Dudley Wheeler, Harold Mansfield, my son John W. Davis, Carrol Coon, Edith Miller, Mr. Higgenbottom and myself — used to go raccoon hunting in the fall.

The coons were numerous around here, killing poultry, damaging corn by pulling down the stalks and eating the ears. They would take only part of an ear, then break off another stalk. They could do an unbearable amount of damage in just one night.

So the boys would come down with their dogs and at about nine o'clock we would start out. We would let the dogs out of the car and they would go down the mile-long road to Osbrook Point. The road went through the fields on one side and the woods on the other. A coon going from the woods to the fields where the corn was would have to cross the road, so the dogs would pick up the track where they had crossed and the fun would begin!

We would follow them down the road in the car with the dogs in the headlights. When they struck a track, we would wait for them to get going. How exciting it was to hear them bay on the track. Each dog had a different tone to his voice and the boys could tell which dog was on the track. They would all run in a pack. The coon would run for the woods and, when the dogs got too close, would climb a tree. Then the baying would become a bark and the boys would say, "He is up!" Then we would go to where the dogs were and flash our lights up into the tree. The coon's eyes would shine in the glow of the light and make a target to shoot at.

Dud Wheeler would have a pistol and could he shoot. He would ask, "Which eye shall I shoot in?" and, when the coon came tumbling down, sure enough, it would be shot in that eye he had named.

Now, it is very easy to get lost in the woods and is especially so on a dark night when we have to go a long distance into the woods to get to the tree where the dogs are barking "up." I remember one night we chased the coon from a cornfield into a swamp going around and around, looking up all the time to locate the coon in the top of the tree. I became so confused I didn't know north from south or any other direction. Dud shot the coon down and seemed as uncertain as I as to how to get back to the cornfield.

Dud took out a cigar, lit it, got it going good and said, "Hear that train? Now, that train is north of us so we must go south to get out of here." He started out that way, the way that I had considered to be wrong, train or no train. Nevertheless, I decided to follow him because I didn't have any direction at all. Dud was right. We soon came to the cornfield and then I realized where we were.

I remember another time when I was tending my traps. I did it in the afternoons as I went on my milk route in the mornings. I was in the woods on the upland and had to cross a swamp to get to the path which I had to take to get home. It had begun to snow and was coming down thick. I turned up the collar of my sheepskin coat, bent my head down and started across the swamp. I jumped from hassock to hassock and soon reached the upland on the other side.

To my amazement, I saw a half cord of wood piled up, then I saw more wood piles, although knowing there was no cord wood cut on that side of the swamp. I was heated as I couldn't figure it out. Then it came to me. I was on the same side of the swamp from which I had started. I had made a complete circle. Then I began all over again but this time I kept my head up and eyes on the upland I was headed for. What a funny feeling it is to be lost. It is like when you wake up in the night and you don't know which side of your bedroom the windows are on or where the door is.

One time, my uncle got lost when a young man. He went crow-nest hunting with intentions to shoot into the nests to break the eggs or kill young crows in the nest. It was a cloudy day so he couldn't tell directions by the sun. He said he wandered around more than two hours before he got out.

Another time, I rode horseback down to the shore by the bay to see if there was enough seaweed for a wagon load. The high tides brought in the seaweed, which we used as bedding for the hogs and cows. Rotted, it made good fertilizer. We valued the seaweed highly.

When I left the shore, I rode toward the road home, going around large clumps of bull briers, through thick woods, etc. The wood lot contained a hundred acres or more. I thought I was taking quite a while to get to the road. Then, I came to an opening where I could see around me good. To my surprise, I was right back on the bay front by the seaweed. Do you know what I did then? I left the bridle reins on the saddle loosely, kicked the horse with my heels and let him find his way out himself. Which he did in no time at all. I think whoever invented the term horse sense knew what he was talking about.

I have broken thirty or thirty-one colts in my life, to drive, ride, or work. When plowing stony ground, sometimes a plow will come in contact with a hidden stone which will top the horses. Now, believe this or not, sometimes the team will slow to almost a crawl and then the plow will fetch up against a hidden flat stone over which the dirt will be four or five inches deep. The horses can somehow feel the stone through the dirt and, knowing that the plow will soon hit the stone, they are ready for it.

I was talking with Dud Wheeler one time and he told me the same thing about his plowing with horses. How they would know and feel those hidden stones and slow down to save themselves a jar on their shoulders when the plow hits the stone.

There have been many serious and fatal accidents with horses but a well-broken and faithful horse on the farm is one of the best friends you can have.

One night, the dogs took a coon track only a little way from the house. We had just turned them loose and they were off. This coon was fast and went a mile before climbing a tree. We could just hear them bark, they were so far away. We drove the car around two miles and down a cart path to get near where the dogs were. The tree was hollow and up about twelve feet from the ground was a place that Dud thought the coon had a nest with young.

Why we didn't shoot the coon I don't know, but we didn't. I think Dud had a young dog with the old one and wanted to have them kill the old coon so he would be more encouraged to hunt. Whit said he would climb in the tree, look in the nest and shake the coon out on the ground. The coon was high above the nest in the top of the tree. Whit called down that there were some young coons in the nest and then he let out a yell.

The coon had decided to come down on the ground and lead the dogs away. She came down over Whit's back, using him as part of the tree trunk, to which he was clinging tightly. She hit the ground and ran between Edith Miller and me, almost knocking us over. Sometime in the past the wind had uprooted a maple tree to whose roots a lot of dirt had clung. Under this pile of roots was a hole which went way under. The coon went into this hole and the dogs couldn't get to her. They tore at the roots and dug with their paws, finally getting to the coon and killing it. The old dog kept opening his mouth, shaking his head and pawing at his face. We couldn't figure out why he did it. Finally, Dud opened the dog's mouth and there was a stick the size of a lead pencil jammed across the roof of his mouth. He had bitten the root off clean and had it stuck between his two sets of teeth. Dud held his mouth open and dislodged the stick and got it out.

Whit was still up in the tree looking at the little coons. There were three of them, so young that they hardly had their eyes open. Dud said that he would like to have them, so he put them in the pocket of his hunting coat and carried them home. He fed them milk by soaking a piece of twisted cloth in warm milk and getting them to suck on this "teat." I guess they were too young to survive with this treatment and he lost all three of them. But was Whit surprised when that coon came climbing down over his back!

There was another fellow who belonged to this group of hunters and with whom I went hunting many times. His name was Latham Miner and he had two good dogs. One was only part hound but he was fast and Late called him Driver. When the two dogs came close to or in sight of the coon, Drive would outrun the hound which was following the track and put the coon "up" very quickly. When Late's dogs got on a track. it was impossible to call them off until they had got the coon up a tree or killed. Sometimes the coon would go into a hole and then the dog would give up. They would search around and look and look but would never bark at the hole. I don't know why they would only bark at the tree.

Sometimes a coon would "tap" a tree. That is, it would go up one tree, and go out on a limb, jump to another tree, and then on to the ground. Off it would go, leaving the dogs barking at the first tree. Those dogs had hunted so much with Late that they knew that when a shot was fired it was the end of the hunt. They figured the coon was killed and that was the end of the hunt for that night. Late would wait around for a while if the dogs couldn't pick up the scent. He would call to them but they wouldn't come. Then Late would fire the gun and the dogs would be there in just a few minutes. I have been hunting with him many times and it always worked.

After hunting, the boys would come back to the house for coffee. Sally, my dear wife, would have a big platter of tunafish sandwiches, two pumpkin pies, and a big pot of Maxwell House coffee on the table. We would sit around the table and tell stories about the other hunts we had had and how smart the dogs were. Each owner's dogs were smarter than the other owners' dogs.

Late said he had a dog one time that was so great a runner that he would catch the coon before the coon could climb the tree. Late said that sometimes he didn't even need to carry a gun, the dog was that good!

Now, when an animal is skinned, be it coon, skunk, muskrat, or any animal whose fur is hide for the fur trade, its hide is stretched on a board to prevent its shrinking when dry. Late said he had a number of different sized boards, each for a different size coon. He said the dog got so good that he would show a board to dog, say, go get him, and the dog would go into the woods and bring back a coon whose hide fit that sized board.

One day, Late decided that he would give the dog a test so he showed him his wife's ironing board. The dog looked at the board and then at Late. Late said, go get him, and the dog went off into the woods. "That," Late said, "was two months ago, but if there is a coon that size anywhere around, that dog will bring him home." He was sure of that.

About roasting a raccoon: First, remove all fat. Every bit of it contains a musk which will taint the meat. Then rub in salt. Rub on a generous amount of poultry seasoning and add six or seven strips of bacon over the meat. Have some water just to cover the bottom of the roasting pan and roast until done. Make a gravy like you would any other roast. Have mashed potatoes and turnips and have yourself a great meal.

One of the hunters liked coffee so well that he complimented my wife on it. He wanted to know what kind it was. We usually used Maxwell House and I guess that probably was the kind we had that night.

He said it reminded him of the city which was holding a convention one time. Every room in the hotel was taken all over the city and there was no place to sleep. Three marines came to this hotel and wanted a room. There was none. They begged for a place to sleep — on chairs, on the floor, anywhere.

The desk clerk said there was a storeroom on the top floor which contained an old bed, couches, etc., which they could use if they wanted to. They gratefully accepted the room and went upstairs.

Then three sailors came in. They had no place to sleep and would stay anywhere just so they could rest. The desk clerk assigned them to the storeroom and they went upstairs. Then three army men came in with the same problem, no place to sleep, and they too went to the storeroom.

Then in came a Red Cross nurse. She had no place to sleep and was all tired out looking for a room. She would be willing to sleep anywhere. The desk clerk told her he only had a storeroom which was partially occupied but she was welcome to use it if she wanted. She said yes and went up to the room.

The next morning down came the three marines. They said they had slept well and thanked him for putting them up for the night. Then they went into the dining room and ordered toast, bacon, eggs, and coffee. Then the three sailors came down. They had slept well too and thanked him for the room. They went into the dining room and ordered toast, bacon, eggs, and coffee. Then the three army men came down. They also thanked him for the room, saying they had slept well. They were very pleased to have had the room. Then they went into the dining room for breakfast, ordering toast, bacon, eggs, and coffee.

Now, said the desk clerk, I am going to prove something. Finally, the Red Cross nurse came in. She was spic and span. Her hair was combed nicely and her uniform was perfect. She thanked him for the room saying she had slept well and was very refreshed. Then she went into the breakfast, ordering toast, bacon and eggs, and tea.

There, said the clerk, that proves something. It proves that nine out of ten prefer coffee.

Jack Graves is a very ardent fox trapper and coon hunter. He is seventy-seven years old and in 1978 he caught thirty-seven fox. Some were red, some gray. They averaged about

$50 per skin. He and a neighbor, Henry Stewart, wondered why the fox they caught were almost always caught by the left front foot. Henry figured it out; they had both used the dirt hole set. At one set, Henry had left a larger amount of dirt at the hole but no track. The dirt was very soft and loose and, of course, the bait was in the hole. The footprints of the fox showed plainly in the soft dirt. The fox must have stood on his left foot and dug out the bait with his right foot, thereby putting all his weight on his left foot. They set the trap where the left foot print showed. The next morning the fox was caught by his left leg.

The trap pan has to be set so it will not trip until the fox puts all his weight on it. The trap also has to be clean and no odor or rust can be on the trap. The trap is cleaned by boiling it in a kettle with wood ashes.

Jack went coon hunting one night with two dogs. One was a dog he had bought in Tennessee which he paid $400 for. The other was just a pup who was beginning to hunt which Jack had raised himself. The old dog took a track and the pup followed along. The wind was blowing hard that night but they could hear the dogs plainly. The chase was quite a long one but finally the dog barked up a tree. Jack and his companion went into the woods towards the tree when suddenly the dogs stopped barking. Jack wondered why they would do that. The dog he had bought was not one to stop barking. He usually would bark all night if no one came to the tree to see the coon. Since the dogs had stopped barking, it was difficult to find the dogs. Jack spent half the night looking for them. He finally gave it up and came home.

The next day, Jack went back to the location and spent most of the day looking for the dogs. They had completely disappeared. Jack came home but the next morning, the pup was in his yard. Somehow, he had found the way home and returned. But no $400 dog. Where that dog was was a mystery.

Time went by, more than a month, when one day Jack went to the mailbox to pick up his mail and there was a letter from a lady from the western part of Connecticut. She had been walking along the road and had seen something in the grass. She picked it up and it was a dog collar with Jack's name and address on the plate, riveted into the leather. Jack had suspected that someone had stolen the dog at the tree, which was why he stopped barking. So Jack was out $400 and a good dog. That is a true story.

Dud Wheeler said he had a dog that he thought was as good as Late Miner's. When Dud went hunting with his dog he would tape up one side of the dog's nose, leaving only one nostril open. When asked why he did this, Dud replied it was so the hound wouldn't chase two coons at once. He could easily have done that if he had a full nose.

One of the hunters said that he had an interesting experience while he was in town. He saw a blind man standing on a street corner waiting to cross over. Thinking to help him across the street, he was approaching when a large police dog trotted up, lifted his leg against the blind man's knees, and soaked him thoroughly down to the shoe. The blind man took a cookie from his pocket and started to feed the dog pieces of the cookie. The hunter asked him why he was feeding that dog, the dog that had just piddled all over his leg. He wanted to know why he was rewarding him. I am not rewarding him, said the blind man. I want to find out which end his head is on so I can kick him in the behind.

When all the sandwiches had been eaten, most of the two pies and two cups of coffee each, one of the hunters got up and asked if twenty-six dogs were coming down the road, what time that would indicate. No one knew. So the hunter said it would be about twenty-five after one and he thought it was about time so he had better get home. So, after shaking hands they all agreed on next Saturday night to go hunting again and they took their departure.

Sally Shaw Davis at the woodstove in the kitchen, one of four in the house. In the middle 1960s, she was still putting up huge quantities of fruits and vegetables for the winter. She also served sandwiches, coffee, and pie to her husband's friends after their raccoon hunts. (Courtesy of Yankee magazine and L. F. Willard)

CHAPTER 21

ABOUT SKUNKS

Uncle John was very fond of skunk meat. So was my father. He would show me where a skunk had been rooting in the meadows for worms. They root up lawns also and are quite a pest around some places. My father would use a small box and enclose part of the front, leaving an opening in which to set a steeltrap. The bait, some old meat, would be placed in the back side in the box and the skunk would have to step into the trap to get it.

How excited I used to get when I saw one in the trap. Father would kill it and how it would smell. I always liked the odor of skunk and I still do. He would have me hold it for him to skin and then he would explain it all out to me so some day I could do it too. He would soak the meat in a pan of water with a little salt added for two days. Then Mother would roast it for him. Mother wouldn't eat any of it herself and I remember well the look on her face when Father gave me my first piece. I ate the whole quarter at one meal.

The oil which fried out of the fat — skunks have lots of fat in the fall to prepare them for hibernation — was carefully saved for medicine. Skunk oil is good for lame joints and to rub on the chest for colds, etc. For hoarseness, Father would mix up skunk's oil and molasses, take a teaspoonful every three to four hours. It seemed to help.

Now, don't confuse the skunk musk with skunk oil. The musk is concentrated in two large glands, located on each side of and at the base of the tail. When attacked, he shoots this musk to defend himself. It is an acid and to counteract it you use baking soda.

Father used to tell about a man who was sick with some kind of a fever. He was so sick the doctor gave him up. An old trapper came to see him and heard the news. He asked would they do anything to try to cure him and break the fever. They said yes. The trapper knew where there was a skunk burrow. He dug it out and brought a live skunk to his friend and put it right on his pillow and left it there. In two days, the fever broke and the man recovered.

One day late in October, Uncle John went to the cider mill with a load of apples to be made into cider. It was Calvin Lee's mill in Wequetequock and he had a boy named Joe. Joe was out to make a dollar wherever he could and used to hunt skunks at nights with a dog. Uncle told him about how he liked skunk and said he never had enough. He said he would give Joe 25 cents for every nicely dressed skunk he could get. Joe promised he would bring them over to him. He said he would be going out after them the first of November. Uncle came home with the cider and didn't think anything more about it.

One day in the middle of November, Uncle was eating his dinner at noon when a team of horses and a wagon drove up to the house. A fellow came to the door and knocked. It was Joe Lee. "Mr. Davis," said Joe, "Do you want some skunks?"

"I sure do," said Uncle. "How many do you have?"

Joe laughed and said he had enough all right. Would Uncle pay him 25 cents for each of them as he said he would? Uncle said yes, of course he would give him twenty-five cents for each and told him to bring them in. There were twenty-five of them. Uncle knew he was caught but he was game and paid $5.25. However, he told Joe he would let them know when he wanted any more.

Some weren't too freshly caught so Uncle threw away seven or eight of them, but Aunt Bess cooked the rest for him and he ate them all.

I am reminded of the old trapper who had some guests from the city visiting him. He was telling them about how he used to set traps for different kinds of animals, how to handle skins, etc. The subject got around to skunks. He extolled the virtues of the skunk, about the fine fur it had, how it hibernated throughout the winter, how its meat was good to eat, and how its oil was used as medicine. Also how penetrating the oil was. His guest expressed disbelief, said he was kidding them about it, and asked if he could prove it was so.

"Watch this," said the old trapper. He then went to a shelf in his cupboard and took down a good-sized bottle of oil. Pouring a quantity on a piece of cloth he smeared a window pane with it, putting on a good thick coat. Waiting fifteen minutes by the clock, he went outside and wiped the window clean. "There, he said, "That's how penetrating it is."

George Chase at his house on the farm. This is where a dozen survivors of the 1938 hurricane who were washed ashore spent a cold, wet night, sustained by the Davises' bread, cider brandy, and ginger tea. The map below, published in the Watch Hill Seaside Topics, *shows the survivors' courses across Little Narragansett Bay to the Davis farm. (Map from the collection of George H. Utter)*

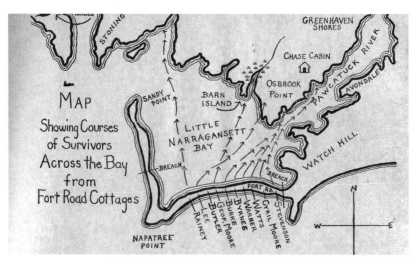

CHAPTER 22

HURRICANE OF 1938 AND STORMS

I delivered the milk as usual on the morning of September 21, 1938. After we had dinner, from twelve o'clock to one o'clock, my hired man and I went out to the barn to put up the pipe on the silo which we were going to start filling the next day. This pipe goes from the cutter to the top of the silo. The wind was blowing so hard we decided to wait until the next day. It was dangerous standing on a ladder twenty-four feet in the air, pulling one end of the pipe up to you in that wind.

I told Cy Havens, who was working here then, to do the chores around the barn and I would go uptown, get a haircut and bring home a plow I had at the blacksmith's shop. My wife, Sally, and sister, Marcia, also decided to go to town, leaving Cy, my son, Whit, Bert Wagner (a boy who was a boarder), and my two aunts — Uncle John's wife, Aunt Bess, and Uncle's sister, Miss Sarah Davis, home.

I got my plow, then had my hair cut. As I left the barber shop, the barber, Joe Grills, said to me, "John, this is a pretty hard blow. See that big cardboard carton going along the sidewalk? It must have come from some department store." When I went out of the shop, I felt the full force of the wind, and I had never seen anything like it. It was difficult to walk. Everything that was loose was blowing along the street or up in the air.

I got into my Ford pickup truck and thought I would get my niece, Jane Hoxie, from the West Broad Street School and take her home to 6 Wilcox Manor where Isabelle, my wife's sister, Mrs. Porter Hoxie, lived. The school was letting out an hour early because of the storm. The rain was coming down in sheets. I got Jane and we made her house all right and went in. Sally was there visiting Isabelle. Isabelle had a Model A Ford sedan, which was parked in the street in front.

As we looked out the window, the pane showed a greenish tinge. Very green. This is the truth. The wind was so hard it was pressing the green leaves against the glass, so hard that the juice from them was running down the window. We looked at each other in disbelief, but it was so.

I said I must go home and see if my aunts were all right. Sally wanted to go too. Isabelle urged us not to go, saying we would be killed by telephone poles or falling trees. Sally insisted on accompanying me, saying that if I was killed, she would die with me. So we started out. That was a ride.

We came down off Wilcox Manor onto West Broad Street, then to Courtland Street. West Broad was blocked there by a large fallen tree. Turning around, I went back up and onto Mayflower Avenue. There on that hill the line of telephone poles were swaying back and forth so as to almost touch the ground. The wires stopped us. I got out of the car, took a small limb which was lying there, and pushed them out of the way.

We went down Palmer Street to William Street where we were again blocked from continuing on Palmer. I went south on William, then up Moss Street and back to Palmer. At the Clark Thread Mill, we were stopped by a guard who warned us not to go past the mill as the boilers were ready to blow at any minute. Seeing the road was clear, I drove as fast as the car would go, which was fast enough. The boilers never did blow, though.

Around the next bend in the road, another tree was clear across and we were blocked completely. I turned around and went up a lane to Clarksville, over into another lane to Mystic Avenue and then back on the main road. No sooner had I turned onto the home road, than another tree blocked us. I told Sally to go to a house for shelter as I didn't think I could get home with the car. We went across a lawn to a fence which I began to help her over. She had climbed part way up when the wind took hold of her and blew her right over it. She landed all in a heap and sprained her ankle.

The house belonged to Jim Rose, and she stayed all night. They were very nice people. Marcia, my sister, stopped at that house also and one of the older boys walked her home about five o'clock that night. I went back to the truck and drove it around a house between some clothes posts, over the lawn and onto the road again where I was obstructed by telephone wires across the road. There was only one thing to do — charge the wires with the truck. They broke and we went through. When I arrived home, there was about fifty feet of telephone wires hanging on the headlights.

I came into the house, went through the dining room and into the sitting room, where my aunts were calmly watching the storm. I tried to open the hall door to go upstairs and couldn't open it. I thought someone was holding it from the other side. It proved to be pressure from the wind, which was building up inside. I finally opened the door and went upstairs to see if there was any damage. The front hall window had blown in. Cy, the boys, and I stopped it as best we could, which wasn't very well. Back in the sitting room, we closed the inside shutters and braced them with a couch and chairs.

We then went to the barns. All the windows and doors were blown off or in. The cupolas were gone and the roof of one silo was off. Cy had wisely put the cows in the barn when it began to rain. Even the covers to holes in the stable gutters had blown up into the stable. The silo, which had not lost its roof, began to wobble as though it would go down any minute. We secured it to the barn by passing the rope through a window and out around the doorway. This we thought would hold it well. It did for a while, then the strain became so great I cut the rope with an ax and down went my silo. But I had saved the barn to which it had been attached.

Bert came running to me then with the news that the sheep barn was gone completely. There were three sheep in the barn at the time and the wind had blown the barn over in the next lot and left them standing there, completely unhurt.

I had built a big storage shed eighty by thirty feet with nice garage doors and I was very proud of it. When Bert told me about the sheep barn, I immediately knew that I would have to keep the flock in that shed for the winter at least. There were fifty sheep and about twenty lambs. Plenty of room, I thought. I was lucky to have that shed. As I came back to the house from the sheep barn I looked at the shed. It was as flat as a pancake.

What next, I thought. I soon found out. A section of the house roof came off with its rafter attached and I don't know to this day where it went. I have never found it. We hurried to the attic with rope and tied down another rafter which was ready to go. This one held and so we saved the roof.

Burton and Whit had a narrow escape from serious injury when the apple tree by the kitchen was torn in half and blown to within six feet of where they were standing one hundred and fifty feet away.

It was now about 3:30 p.m. and we began to think of milking. We were without electricity and there would be no lights in the barn that night. We had milked two or three of the eighteen we had to do when one of the boys burst in all excited. He could see a house down on the flat land by the river. We all looked then and saw not only a house down but water four or five feet high coming toward us in big waves.

A tidal wave, I said. I had heard of such things but I had never expected to see one. It was headed for our only supply of drinking water, the spring at the foot of the hill. We hurriedly dumped what milk we had in the pails and grabbed anything that would hold water. We rushed to the spring and filled them all and brought them to the house. The water came across the road which leads to Osbrook but didn't quite get to the spring well. When I saw that the danger of that was passed, we went back to milking.

About this time my sister arrived home and I was very glad to see her. My two aunts were alone in the house and what was going on was too incredible but they were not the least bit afraid.

We were almost finished with the milking when Marcia came up to the barn with the news that a young woman was down at the house, saying she had just come up from Osbrook. Her name was Mrs. Irma Nurmi and she was a maid in the house of Mr. Ronald M. Byrnes, a summer resident of Watch Hill. She said Mr. Byrnes was down there too and she didn't know how he was getting on. Cy and I saddled up a young horse which my son Whit had trained to swim in the Pawcatuck River for fun. She wasn't afraid of the water. The water had begun to recede from the higher places by now and Cy went on foot with boots. We met Mr. Byrnes about one quarter mile down the Osbrook Road. Cy and I got him on the horse and brought him up and helped him into the house. He was cold and bushed out and wanted me to call an ambulance to take him to the Westerly Hospital. He didn't realize the wires were all down. I told him he would have to stay with me all night.

He agreed and we put him to bed. I covered him heavily with blankets to get him warm. Marcia had put the girl to bed and she seemed to be all right. We were afraid to light the wood cooking stove because of fire. We boiled the tea kettle on a small oil stove and made them good hot tea. I had some cider brandy which I added to the tea and it really made a warm drink. Mr. Byrnes said he liked the kind of tea we made but his feet were cold. We got some more hot water, filled a rubber hot water bottle with it and placed it in the bed against his feet. When the heat touched his cold flesh, it caused the muscles in his legs to go into spasms which were very painful. We rubbed the muscles until they returned to normal and took away the hot water bottle.

Then George Chase came up through the water and debris wearing hip boots. He said he had a dozen or so in the cabin and wanted something to eat. He wanted above all other things some ginger to make them hot ginger tea. I gave him a loaf of bread, some cider brandy and a box of ginger. Thinking there might be more down there wandering around in the dark,

Burt and I saddled up two horses, took flashlights and went down to see if we could find anyone. We didn't but I think it was our flashlights which the Geoffrey Moore family saw from Barn Island as we went around that way and kept flashing the lights.

The next morning George's guests were all taken home. Mr. Byrnes went to stay with Mr. Charles Sherman, a friend of his. Mr. Byrnes was a nice man; he had lost his two daughters and his wife in the hurricane.

What a long, hard job we had building things back. The first thing we did was to set the outdoor toilet back up and get it ready for business. That was first. Second was to obtain ice for the milk room so we could cool the milk. My truck started good and I went up to the ice plant in Avondale for a cake. They let me have it as I had to keep food. On my way home I brought Sally back and thanked the Rose family for their kindness to us.

I sent my son, Whit, with the milk that morning. He drove his horse Queen in the express wagon and carried an ax and saw with him to clear away the tree tops through which he had to pass in several places. I stayed home to repair the house roo,f which we finished before it rained again.

The trees had lost all their leaves and the woods looked as they do in December, all bare.

By spring, thanks to two good friends of mine, Jesse Cornell and Harold Fallon, we had built a new sheep barn, repaired the barns and also the shed. Then we went to work on the debris around the walls and in the meadows. Jess found a house and we hauled the sides and ends down to his lot and set it up by the river on Greenhaven. We found the house sections by the color of the paint, which was green, and they all fitted together. So Jesse got a home out of it.

Besides that hurricane, we used to have some severe storms. I had to be out in them to deliver the milk each day. Some were rain, some were snow. In the winter, with the thermometer down around ten degrees above zero and a high wind blowing, it was trying work.

I began my milk route in the fall of 1921. I had a pickup truck which I used to go to Watch Hill in the summer. I would use it until January 1, then peddle the milk through January, February, and March with a horse and wagon. The wagon I used the first three winters was an open express wagon and I had no shelter from the storms. All the old milkmen, before they got trucks, had an enclosed wagon with sliding doors and glass windows. The reins from the horse came through two holes in the front. The horse had a rain-proof blanket which kept it quite dry and warm.

My neighbor Russell Stewart, who sold milk retail about five years before I began, had such an outfit. On cold days, he and the other boys who delivered their milk carried a lantern in the wagon for warmth. This doesn't seem like much, but it helped quite a bit.

Before bottles came into fashion, milk was carried in ten-quart cans and was measured out in quarts to the customers, who would leave their pitchers or other containers on their doorsteps to be filled. They would be covered over with a dish or saucer.

The story goes that one milkman who was a little careless about things was surprised to find two pitchers out one morning. He knocked on the door and asked why two pitchers that day, did the woman want both filled. His customer replied, "Yes. Put the dirt in one pitcher and the milk in the other." So that was that.

On another occasion, a milkman had his young son helping deliver that day. The boy put the milk in the pitcher and was replacing the cover when the door opened and the lady of the house appeared. She told the boy that yesterday she discovered a small frog in the pitcher of milk and she wondered why. The boy said his father had strained the milk the night before but had probably forgotten to strain the water, which was a very good explanation.

Now, here is an actual fact. During the war many young couples were shifted around to different cities and towns where the young husband was in service. He would be stationed four or five months in one place, then transferred to another. They were very nice people. I had one such couple on my route and when payday came around I stopped for the money. I knocked on the door and the lady came out with some bills in her hand. We made change as best we could but I had to give her a dime instead of a nickel. She was going back upstairs for the five cents when I stopped her.

"Don't bother," I said. "You needn't go up just for a nickel. Put it in the baby's bank."

She looked thoughtful for a moment, then said, "I guess it is a little early yet as I am only two months along."

I always kept a sleigh ready for a big snow because I couldn't get the car through the drifts. After the third winter, I ran a Model T Ford and kept it going all winter. They were high off the ground, had narrow wheels and went through the snow and mud like nobody's business, which was easy. Many a time I drove around cars of other makes which were stuck hopelessly in the snow. There were no town trucks with snow plows in those days and we had to shovel the roads out by hand. The roads were all dirt.

After a big snow, the whole neighborhood would turn out with shovels, meet at some appointed place, and work as one unit under one boss. We could usually clear the Lower Pawcatuck area in one day. Howard Brown was boss. We would give him a list of the number of hours we worked and he would send the bill to the town. When he got the money, he would pay us off. We would visit with one another while working but everybody kept shoveling. When the drifts were shoulder high, we would put a path through only wide enough for a one horse team to pass. Knee high or so, we would open it right up. How pretty the world was after a big storm, all white and clean, clear and cold, the sun shining on the whiteness to make you a little snowblind. What fun it was to work that way with friends and neighbors.

Now, before the roads were cleared the milk had to go through and be delivered to our customers in the morning. I remember one big storm the winter of 1926-27. It began to snow about six o'clock in the evening with a high northeast wind blowing hard. It blew and snowed all night. I got my hired man up at 4:30 a.m. We went to the barn and did the milking. We always milked at 5 a.m. but on stormy mornings I got up half an hour earlier to fight the storm. The snow was so deep we couldn't drive the Model T so I decided to take the express wagon and drive Daisy, my best horse. Daisy was a bay mare and the most reliable animal that ever lived. I have thought many times, what would I do without her. I bought her when Sally and I were first married and she was almost a member of the family. She was tough and strong and a most willing worker. Leslie harnessed Daisy and loaded in the crates of milk while I ate my breakfast.

I bundled up well, got in, spread the thick horse blanket over my legs, and we started off. Thinking the river road would be blocked with drifts, I decided to go to the Schoolhouse Road. It was blowing and snowing so hard as we reached the top of the hill past the cemetery that I could not see the walls beside the road and hardly the mare's tail. I gave her a loose rein and let her choose her own way. She kept the middle of the road, but I don't know how she did it.

When we got to the corner of the road by Schiller's house, she stopped still. I couldn't see what was the matter because of the smothering snow so I yelled, "Get up!" She reared and jumped ahead, breaking the whipple tree. I called "whoa" and she stopped. I saw she was in a drift up to her chest. I got down from the wagon, unhitched her and we wallowed our way through the drift. The wagon stayed there three days before it was dug out by the road gang. On the other side of the corner, the wind had blown the road nearly clear. We went through a barway into a field back to the road again and home.

Leslie had just finished his breakfast. We got out the sleigh, took a coal shovel and rode back to the stalled wagon. We transferred the milk to the sleigh and, with me leading Daisy and Leslie walking behind to keep the sleigh from tipping over, we did the whole milk route that way. We got home at three o'clock in the afternoon. The next day, I went alone with

Combined operation: the Davises and their neighbors, the Russell Stewarts, joined forces after a storm in 1949 to deliver their milk by sled. (Photos courtesy of the Stewart family)

the sleigh and the road had been dug out to the schoolhouse from the river. When I arrived home from the milk route, I took Sally and Whit for a sleigh ride. I have a picture of them in the sleigh with Daisy.

When the town blacktopped all the roads, bought heavy equipment, and put the highway department on the job working all night to keep the roads clear, we had a much easier time of it as far as travel was concerned. We milkmen had to be out in all kinds of weather but it was much faster and more comfortable with a truck. The cab could be heated and would be warm. I never had a heater in my car as it somehow seemed to give me a cold. If I rode with someone who had a heater, I would always ask them to turn it off. Then again, if you wore heavy clothing, you would feel the cold more when you got out of the car, so I didn't have one.

The winter of 1933-34 was one of the coldest I have ever known. The thermometer went down to twenty-six degrees below zero and, with more than a foot of snow on the ground, it didn't go above freezing for six weeks. When it did, it seemed almost like summer by comparison. I had a Model A Ford. We would pour hot water in the manifolds and it would start right up. They were good cars.

The last day of February 1949, we had a big snowstorm. The snow was so deep and drifted that we couldn't get out of the yard with a car. I telephoned my neighbor Russell Stewart, to see how he was making out and he couldn't get out of his yard either. The roads weren't cleared yet and he didn't know what to do. I told him I had a big wood sled and a team that was hard. They hadn't been laid up through the winter to get out of condition. I said I would hitch them to the wood sled, load my milk, go over to his house, take his milk on and we would deliver together. He agreed and over we went. His yard was drifted so badly he had to put one of his horses on ahead of my two to get up his hill. We loaded on the milk and went uptown with it. He and I had customers on the same streets so we put the milk out in no time. We then went to the grain store and got some hundred-pound bags of grain and came home. That was the last time we peddled with the horses. I have a picture taken of us on the way home.

The Stewarts were nice people and many a nice supper Sally and I have had with them at their house. Then they would come over here and have supper. I used to meet Russ on the milk route almost every day and we would stop and talk and exchange the news. I miss them very much.

When the roads thawed out in the spring, they really were muddy. One time, I got stuck in the mud on the way home with my truck. I had on the empty bottles, cases, and grain. I had to walk home and get the team to pull me out. They did it easily. The truck's rear end housing was dragging in the mud.

Sally and John Lawrence Davis and their son, Whit, riding a sleigh pulled by the mare Daisy at Willow Tree Cove on the Pawcatuck River, probably in the big freeze of 1934, when the temperature dropped to –26 degrees.

In 1971, L. F. Willard, a writer for Yankee *magazine, visited the Davis Farm, where three generations were at work: John Lawrence Davis (at right) and Sally; their son, John Whitman Davis, and his first wife, Hazel, and their 14-year-old son, Lawrence Malcolm Davis. The two older men are in the farmyard with Larry, next to his father. (Courtesy of* Yankee *magazine and L. F. Willard)*

Whit Davis puts out hay and water for the cows. Below, Larry Davis herds cows with the help of neighbors. (Courtesy of Yankee *magazine and L. F. Willard)*

Larry Davis at the North Stonington Fair with his prize calves. His grandfather John Lawrence Davis and father, John Whitman Davis, observe. (Courtesy of Yankee *magazine and L. F. Willard)*

CHAPTER 23

THE SEASONS

I was just sitting here by the dining room window when a gust of wind came whistling through the keyhole of the kitchen door. How Sally and I used to look forward to the sound of wind through the keyhole in the fall.

It meant the end of the hot, sultry, and muggy weather of the dog days. Now that the air was clear and cool and you could really get your breath, how nice it was. Most of all it meant that fall was here, the time of harvest and the getting ready for the long cold winter ahead. The birds were now gathering together in flocks for their long flight south. Soon they would be gone. How still it would be without them.

We also knew the frosts were soon to be, only hoping that they wouldn't be to soon and kill the summer squash, tomatoes, corn, etc. The first frost would be a white one; that is, it would kill in the lower spots and not the entire plant. Later would come the black frost. This was a real freeze that would leave the plants black and dead. The black frost would usually appear around the tenth of October.

Regarding sweet corn, after a black frost, you can still pick the ears even though the leaves have gone white. The stalk will keep juice in the kernels for two or more weeks. We would always try to get our field corn, the johnnycake corn, cut and shucked before frost because that was the plant that we fed to the cattle through the winter. It was husked, bound in small bundles, and stacked. The field corn was ready to cut when the kernels began to glaze over. This was about the fourteenth of September.

Following the corn would come the digging of the potatoes. By the time the potatoes were in the cellar, the corn would be dry enough to begin the husking. If the potatoes were rotting then they would be left in the ground until they got through rotting. This was about the middle or last of October. The late blight is what makes them rot. If put in the cellar in that condition, it will surely be a mess as they will continue to rot. In the fields, the potatoes are separated by the soil so they are kept clean.

November was the time the winter supply of firewood was brought home. It had been cut and piled in the woods last winter so it would dry out and season. It was then sawed into stove length pieces and split. In order to keep the stoves going all winter, it required about twenty cords of wood. The woods available were maple, red, and white oak and hickory. All these except the white oak made quick hot fires. The white oak burned more slowly and lasted longer. The white oak was good to bank a fire to last all night. It was best in an airtight stove that required large sticks.

October was one of my favorite months. The leaves would be so wonderfully colored and the goldenrod and purple asters were so pretty. I used to gather the asters and the goldenrod and put them on the fireplace for as long as they would keep.

We used to plant pumpkin seeds in the cornfields between the hills of corn, about six feet apart. After the corn was shucked, we would gather the pumpkins and store them in the barn. When it got too cold, we would put them in the cellar. We would have from four to six tipcart loads of them. They were either boiled or mixed with skim milk so they could be fed to the hogs. This made pretty good hog feed. We would also crush them with a big wooden maul and feed them to the cows and calves we were raising. The animals did well on it.

On the tenth of November, we would pull the winter turnips, which had been planted about the twentieth of July. Somewhere between twenty-five and two hundred bushel of turnips were pulled depending on how well they had done. What we didn't sell were chopped into small pieces with a spade and fed to the cows. Some were also boiled for the pigs. The pigs didn't seem to relish them very much but we mixed them with other feed and they helped out.

Apples were picked on the first of October. The picked fruit was carefully stored in barrels and bushel baskets down cellar. The cellar window and door were left open for fresh air to circulate until December.

The carrots and the beets were also pulled and tapped in November. The ground usually froze about the middle of November but the carrots, beets, and turnips would freeze in and then thaw out while in the ground. It is claimed that freezing in the ground makes them sweeter. Before the next freeze, you should pull them right away as the next freeze may be the one to last all winter. I would set eight hundred to a thousand cabbage plants, Danish Bald Head, in June. It would yield four or five hundred nice heads. I would store some in the barn and two hundred and fifty down cellar. We wouldn't eat that many, but what we didn't eat went to the pigs and the poultry.

The eleventh of November was hog butchering time, provided the moon was on the rise. If it wasn't, then as soon as it was. The moon affects the quality of the meat, makes it sweeter, and it keeps better.

Daylight savings time ended the last Sunday in October. We looked forward to the fall change as it meant the long winter evenings to enjoy. It shortened the day's work but we looked upon it as vacation time. We still had plenty of chores but no field work then. We worked in the woods and at the woodpile, splitting the sawed pieces for the stoves. We would work until about four o'clock.

We would then start the night chores by feeding the sheep, watering and feeding the horses (we had about twelve horses and colts), milking the cows, and feeding them and their calves.

The wood boxes were always filled before night in case of a storm. The wood would then be dry for the next day. If the wood was wet, we would pile some on the back of the kitchen stove to dry and sometimes in the oven. I've kept a few finely split sticks on the back of the stove at all times. I mix it with the larger pieces of wood when the fire is low and it catches fire more quickly.

Sometimes, when we came in for supper there would be radiant sunset and sometimes there would be a sundog. Sundogs are bright spots, either on the side or above the setting sun. They are a sign of a storm. We used to call such a sunset a storm sunset as it usually stormed the second day after. Sally loved these gorgeous sunsets, as did I. We would stand on the walk by the door, hold hands and think of what a beautiful world it was. Then we would kiss each other.

While she was getting supper, I would finish filling the wood box. Everybody would come in then for supper and wash their hands at the sink. Each had his own towel and we always washed face and hands before supper. There were nine of us at the table: my two aunts, two hired men, my sister, Whit, a boy who boarded with us, Sally and I. The boy's parents were divorced and each visited him separately so as not to come in contact with each other. He paid $5 per week to Sally. That was her money to do with as she liked. Needless to say, she spent it wisely.

How nice to come in out of the cold and relax where it was warm. What comfort it was to know that the stock were well fed and comfortable in the barn for the night. Then we would all sit down at the table there for supper. There was always plenty to eat and plenty to spare. Most things we ate came directly off the farm. Baked beans, johnnycakes, potatoes (we had them three times a day), mashed turnips, creamed onions, cornbread, pepper relish to go with the beans, our own homemade butter, and cabbage salads. Another time it might be roast duck with stuffing, mashed potatoes, mashed turnips, boiled onions, cranberry sauce from our own cranberry bog. We used to have two bushels of cranberries for the winter.

Other meals would be corned beef, dried beef gravy, egg sauce, chicken with biscuits, potatoes served different ways,

Harvard beets, creamed carrots, corn pudding, and just about everything you could think of. For desserts, we had apple cake or pie, cranberry-raisin or pumpkin pie. This is the way we ate all the time. And to think it all came off the farm. Sally was a most wonderful cook.

When supper was finished, we all carried our plates and silverware into the kitchen. This saved Sally many steps when cleaning off the table. The hired men would go to their room for the evening and I would get the popcorn out. We always had popcorn and apples in the evening.

While Sally was doing the dishes I would shell some of the corn into the popper. I would hold it over the coals in the sitting room stove. The corn popper had to be kept in motion or else it would burn. You also had to be careful that it was not too full or that too would burn. It takes some practice to judge just the right amount of heat to pop the corn properly.

Sally melted some butter on the stove. When I had a pan full of popped corn, I would take it into the kitchen and Sally would season it with the butter and salt. She could do it just right. When we had guests, how they loved the popcorn. We raised the old-fashioned (bear paw) or white rice popcorn. The skin is very tender, more so than other kinds of popcorn. We had small bowls to serve it in.

I took several farm magazines: The Rural New Yorker, Country Gentleman, New England Homestead, Farm Journal, a horse magazine, and a poultry paper. Sally had Better Homes and Gardens, Saturday Evening Post, and two other magazines. We also subscribed to the daily newspaper.

She sat on one side of the table and I the other, reading our newspapers and eating popcorn. When the corn was almost gone or we had had enough, I would get the dish of apples from the hall. I would quarter one, remove the core, peel it and hand it to her. After we had an apple or two, Sally would go upstairs and light the stove in our bedroom. That way it would be warm when we went to bed. She would go into my sister's room to watch Lawrence Welk and listen to an hour of music. My sister had a television and we only had a radio.

At nine o'clock, Sally would come downstairs to put away the washed dishes from supper and lock the door, etc. We used to joke about putting out the cat (we didn't own a cat). It would be so cozy in the sitting room that we would linger there for a while before going upstairs.

Our bedroom was small and warm and cozy too. We would lie there under the blankets and watch the flame in the stove flicker on the ceiling. We were warm and comfortable; how happy we were. Sometimes, it would be storming and I would shine the flashlight out the window. I would flash it toward the chimney to see how hard it was snowing. On stormy mornings, I would get up and call the boys at 4:30 a.m. instead of the usual 5 a.m. Things went more slowly on snowy days and we were sure to have to dig to the garage to get the milk truck. I delivered every morning I wasn't sick for forty-six years.

Sally and I would take a trip off for two days in October. We liked to go to Vermont, New Hampshire, and Maine. What a treat that was. The longest trip that we took ever was to Vermont in 1926.

We all worked as a way of life in those days and thought nothing of it. One boy stayed with me for eight years and never asked for a day off all those years. His name was Jim Anderson; this was his home.

CHAPTER 24

IF YOU KEEP THE LAND
THE LAND WILL KEEP YOU

I used to keep three brood sows and a boar. The sows were bred to pig in March and April and the piglets were sold when eight or ten weeks old. There used to be quite a demand for them.

One year, we had an order for four pigs to go to Block Island. The man sent us a check and they were to be sent over on the ferry from Point Judith. We used two crates, two pigs to a crate, and went down to Point Judith to ship them off. We had never been there before but found the dock and the ferry. The boat was being loaded with cars and other freight and the captain said to wait a little while and he would load the pigs. We waited by the truck for him to be ready.

There were other boats at the dock, most of them fishing boats. There was a man standing by one of them smoking a pipe. He came over to our truck to see the pigs and get acquainted. He wanted to know about the farm and how we made a living.

We explained that milk was our major source of income, that we produced it from our own herd, bottled it, and sold it retail. We sold about one hundred quarts per day. However, the milk just about paid the grain bill and for the running of the farm, the help, repairs, etc. I told him I had two men by the month, room and board.

Now I said we have other means of getting money which we called cash crops. Now those pigs for instance. We had three good brood sows which had done very well that spring. They raised thirty-two pigs which we sold for $30 each, $960 total but not all profit, however. We bought grain from the grain store but we fed them mostly from the farm with such food as skimmed milk, small potatoes, squash, turnip, sweet corn, garbage from the house, etc. We also raised strawberries, which that year yielded us $300. We also sold many vegetables on our milk route. All in all we got by the best we could.

We lived mostly from the farm. We have two gardens, one for summer and one for winter. The summer vegetables are spinach, peas, string beans, squash, cucumbers, tomatoes, sweet corn, etc. Also beets and carrots. The winter garden is potatoes, turnip, winter squash, field beans for baking, cabbage, pumpkin, onions, etc.

We have one hundred and twenty-five hens. We raise two hundred chickens every spring, sell and eat the roosters in the fall and keep the pullets for laying. We have geese and ducks too. We butcher two pigs, about two hundred pound, each November. That gives us salt pork for chowder and to bake in the beans, ham and bacon all winter. In January, we butcher a beef, an old cow or bull. Some goes into the brine for corned beef and some hangs in the corn crib for soups. Some is brined and smoked for dried beef gravy. Of course, we have our own smoke house.

We also raise three or four hundred bushel of flint corn which we have ground into meal for johnnycakes. My wife does a lot of canning in the summer for our winter use.

This is what I told the man at the dock. And as I have always said, and I maintain, that if you keep the land the land will keep you.

Sally and John Lawrence Davis were married for 57 years. When she died in 1979, he wrote: "She was a wonderful girl, loved the Farm and always helped me in every way."

This book was set in
Century Schoolbook
(True Type), a typeface
originally created for the
Century magazine by
Linn Boyd Benton and
redesigned by his son,
Morris Fuller Benton, to
serve as the type used in
millions of schoolbooks.

Printing by Maple-Vail
Manufacturing Group of
York, Pennsylvania.